MEXICAN COOKING

BY
CYNTHIA SCHEER

ILLUSTRATED BY DAVID REDMOND

OWLSWOOD PRODUCTIONS

Book and Cover Design: Dennis Redmond

Location Photography: Cynthia Scheer

Editor: Susan H. Herbert

TABLE OF CONTENTS

ABOUT THE AUTHOR

Cynthia Scheer is a professional food consultant and free-lance writer on food, wine and travel. She received her degree in Home Economics from Michigan State University. (In 1970, the University honored her with a Distinguished Alumni Award.) She has been a food editor of *Sunset Magazine,* writes a food column for *Chevron USA* and has written for *Sphere* and *Gourmet* magazines. Her cookbooks for Owlswood Productions include BRAVO! ITALIAN COOKING, FRENCH COUNTRY FAVORITES and GERMAN HOME COOKING.

No armchair cook, Ms. Scheer prefers to learn about the food of a country or region by spending as much time as possible seeing and tasting the products of its markets, restaurants, street vendors, bakeries and home kitchens. "There is something about a market—even a supermarket," she believes, "that helps to place individual dishes in context. I like to see what fruits and vegetables are grown in a region and taste the wine or beer of that region. Almost invariably, they enhance each other."

Her investigation of Mexican cooking for this book has taken place over a number of years, with repeated visits to Mexico City, as well as to popular beach resorts on the West and Caribbean coasts. She also spent time in the states of Yucatán, Oaxaca and Jalisco—all noted for their distinctive food specialties.

Born and educated in Wisconsin and Michigan, Ms. Scheer now lives in the San Francisco Bay Area, a convenient starting point for enjoying the colorful cooking of Mexico.

PREFACE

Living in California and traveling in Mexico and the Southwestern United States have provided a joyous education for my Midwestern palate. Mexican cooking, though it can differ vastly in all these areas, takes flamboyant advantage of the ingredients it finds at hand. In Mexico that means a colorful spectrum of spices and herbs, lushly ripe tropical fruits, a veritable cornucopia of vegetables, the freshest of fish and seafoods—and a delight in making the most ingenious use of all of them.

The recipes in this book recreate some fondly recollected Mexican dishes from many places: beach resorts where tourists flock, sophisticated cities such as Mexico City and Guadalajara, and also modest places where the tortillas were irresistibly warm and the beer equally cold. Many recipes are modeled after favorite dishes in Mexican restaurants in California, Arizona, Texas and New Mexico.

It was of first importance in developing the recipes to achieve genuinely Mexican-tasting dishes using ingredients *you* can find readily at hand. After all, the oldest aspects of the Mexican kitchen are such familiar things as corn, tomatoes, beans and chocolate—all native to this hemisphere. If you live in the West or Southwest, you should have no difficulty finding what you need to prepare any of the recipes in this book. Elsewhere in the United States and Canada, you may have to seek out supermarkets or specialty stores that feature products especially for Mexican cooking.

IT BEGINS WITH THE TORTILLA

At the very heart of Mexican cooking is the *tortilla*. Walking down a street in a Mexican town at mid-day, one smells the aroma of the flat little ground corn pancakes toasting on stone griddles and hears the rhythmic sound of them being patted and slapped into thin rounds.

As anyone who has ever enjoyed a taco or an enchilada knows, however, although a tortilla (say *tor*-TEE–*ah*) is made from a kind of corn meal, the flavor bears no resemblance to north-of-the-border corn bread or muffins.

That's because the corn from which tortillas, tamales and many other Mexican foods are made is treated in an entirely different way—soaking the kernels in lime water, then grinding them finely in a stone mortar. In many households in Mexico, tortillas are still made in this way, with the corn ground in the traditional stone mortar or *metate*.

When you make tortillas to serve as a warm bread or to use as the basis for dishes such as tacos and tostadas, use packaged corn tortilla flour or *masa harina*. It is sold in 5- and 10-pound bags and needs only the addition of water to make fresh corn tortillas.

Recipes in this cookbook were tested with both homemade and commercially made tortillas. The latter are available in California, the Southwest and in areas with a substantial Mexican-American population. They can be purchased fresh or in refrigerated packages or in cans. The flavor and texture of packaged tortillas and those you make at home are somewhat different, but they can be used interchangeably.

Corn Tortillas

2   cups *masa harina* (packaged
     corn tortilla flour)
1¼   cups warm water

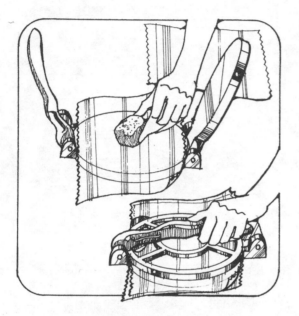

Mix *masa harina* and warm water in a bowl, stirring until the mixture is well blended and pulls away from the sides of the bowl. With your hands, shape it into a ball, then divide into 15 or 16 equal pieces.

To form tortillas, flatten each piece of dough and place it between squares of waxed paper in center of tortilla press. Lower top of press, taking care not to wrinkle paper. Press down firmly on lever until the tortilla measures 5-1/2 to 6 inches in diameter. Carefully remove the top sheet of waxed paper. Stack tortillas (on bottom pieces of waxed paper) until ready to cook.

To cook tortillas, heat a well seasoned (but ungreased) griddle over moderately high heat until water sprinkled over the surface dances in droplets. Invert the tortilla, paper-side up, onto the griddle. When tortilla becomes warm, peel off the paper. Cook, turning frequently with tongs, a small spatula or your fingers, until the tortilla looks dry and is lightly flecked with brown specks. Stack cooked tortillas in a pan until ready to use. Serve warm, with butter, or wrap tightly and refrigerate or freeze. Makes 15 to 16 tortillas, 5-1/2 to 6 inches in diameter.

The Tortilla Press

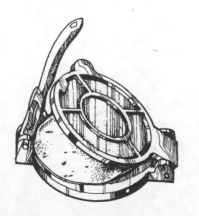

One probably could learn to pat tortillas out by hand, but it is a laborious task. A far easier way to shape tortillas uniformly is to use a tortilla press. Made of heavy metal, the press flattens a ball of corn tortilla dough into a thin round when you use the lever to bring the two metal disks together. To prevent the tortilla from sticking to the press, place the ball of dough between squares of waxed paper. The paper can be reused one or more times after the tortilla is transferred to a griddle to bake.

In Mexican markets you may also find a hinged wooden tortilla press. It works on the same principle, using two square wooden plates.

The Tortilla Griddle

Whether you are going to eat tortillas just spread with butter, or use them in some other dish for which they will be fried, you must first cook the tortillas on a griddle. The important thing in choosing the griddle is to find one that is large enough. Corn tortillas usually are 5-1/2 to 6 inches in diameter, and flour tortillas (see page 28) are even larger. A big griddle will enable you to cook two or more at a time, speeding up the process.

In Mexico the flat earthenware griddle used for cooking tortillas is a *comal,* and you can still find them in many Indian markets.

Like an omelet or crêpe pan, a tortilla griddle serves better if it is well seasoned. Nonstick coatings are fine, but not necessary for making tortillas. Brush the cooking surface of a new griddle evenly with salad oil, then place it over low heat for about 15 minutes. When the griddle cools, rub off excess oil with a paper towel.

If you use the griddle only for tortillas and pancakes, it should not need washing after each use; just wipe away crumbs. Using your tortilla griddle in between for grilled sandwiches (buttering the bread on the outside) will help to season it. If you find tortillas beginning to stick, season the griddle again. With repeated use, your griddle will acquire a golden brown patina—and your tortillas will *never* stick!

One of the easiest ways to get acquainted with Mexican food is by trying a *taco* (say TAH-*co*). Sometimes described as a Mexican sandwich, it is true that tacos can contain practically any food you like. And the more you cram into the crisp fried tortilla shell, the more fun a taco is to eat. You can buy packaged taco shells, already fried and ready to use, but those you make at home taste much better.

These tacos have a tomato and chicken filling and a typical California topping of shredded lettuce and cheeses. Add hot sauce to taste.

Chicken Tacos, California Style

3 halved chicken breasts
    (about 1½ lbs.)
1 can (14½ oz.) sliced baby
    tomatoes
1 medium onion, chopped
1 small can (4 oz.) green chiles,
    seeded and chopped
1 teaspoon garlic salt
½ teaspoon *each* chile powder
    and crumbled oregano
    Oil for deep frying
12 corn tortillas, softened (see page 22)
    Shredded iceberg lettuce (2 to 3 cups)
¾ cup *each* shredded Monterey jack
    and Cheddar cheeses, mixed
    Canned green chile salsa
    (optional)

Place chicken breasts in a frying pan. Top with tomatoes and their liquid, onion, chiles, garlic salt, chile powder and oregano. Bring to boiling, cover, reduce heat and simmer for 30 minutes, until chicken is tender. Remove chicken from sauce, and when it is cool enough to handle, remove and discard bones and skin. Meanwhile, bring sauce to boiling and cook quickly, stirring frequently, until liquid is reduced and sauce is thick. Return chicken, shredded in bite-sized pieces, to sauce. Cover and keep warm. (*Or* make ahead, refrigerate, then reheat.)

To prepare taco shells, pour oil to a depth of at least 1 inch into a heavy frying pan, electric skillet or Chinese wok; heat to 370°. Fold tortillas in half and, holding them at top edge with tongs, place one at a time in the hot oil; use tongs to keep tortillas folded and hold top edges apart. Fry, turning once or twice, until crisp and lightly browned. Drain, and remove to paper towels to complete draining. Keep taco shells warm in a 200° oven until ready to assemble.

Fill fried taco shells with chicken mixture, then top with shredded lettuce and cheeses. Serve with green chile salsa to taste. Makes 4 to 6 servings.

The filling for these beef tacos derives much of its flavor from the *chorizo* sausage (say *chore*-EAT-*so*). These spicy red pork sausages are used extensively in Mexican cooking. If you can't obtain them, you might substitute an equal weight of Portuguese-style *linguiça* or hot Italian-style pork sausage.

California Beef and Chorizo Tacos

2   chorizo sausages (about 6 oz.)
1   pound ground beef, crumbled
1   medium onion, chopped
1   clove garlic, minced or pressed
1   can (8 oz.) tomato sauce
¼   teaspoon ground cumin
¼   cup halved ripe olives
    Oil for deep frying
12 corn tortillas
    Shredded iceberg lettuce (2 to 3 cups)
1½ cups shredded Monterey jack
      cheese
    Canned green chile salsa

Remove casings and crumble chorizos into a large frying pan. Cook the sausage over medium heat in its own drippings for about 5 minutes, stirring occasionally. Add ground beef, about one-fourth at a time, cooking and stirring until browned. Spoon off excess fat. Add onion and garlic, and cook until tender. Mix in tomato sauce, cumin and olives. Bring to boiling, cover, reduce heat and simmer for 30 minutes. Uncover, and boil gently until liquid is reduced and sauce is thick, stirring frequently. Keep meat mixture warm. (*Or* make ahead, refrigerate, then reheat.)

To prepare taco shells, pour oil to a depth of at least 1 inch into a heavy frying pan, electric skillet or Chinese wok; heat to 370°. Soften tortillas if they are not freshly made (see page 22). Fold soft tortillas in half and, holding them at top edge with tongs, place one at a time in the hot oil; use tongs to keep tortillas folded and hold top edges apart. Fry, turning once or twice, until crisp and lightly browned. Drain, and remove to paper towels to complete draining. Keep taco shells warm in a 200° oven until ready to assemble.

Fill fried taco shells with meat mixture, then top with shredded lettuce and cheese. Serve with green chile salsa to taste. Makes 4 to 6 servings.

To test the assertion that anything tastes better when it's inside a taco, try these refreshing Tuna Tacos. They are a marvelous quick lunch or spur-of-the-moment supper with beer or soft drinks.

Tuna Tacos

1   can (6½ oz.) chunk light tuna, drained and flaked
1   small tomato, chopped
2   green onions, sliced (include tops)
    Dash garlic salt
    Oil for deep frying
8   corn tortillas, softened (see page 22)
2   cups shredded iceberg lettuce
1½ tablespoons Italian-style bottled dressing
1   cup shredded Cheddar cheese
    Canned green chile salsa

For filling, lightly mix tuna, tomato, onions and garlic salt. To prepare taco shells, pour oil to a depth of at least 1 inch into a heavy frying pan, electric skillet or Chinese wok; heat to 370°. Fold tortillas in half and, holding them at top edge with tongs, place one at a time in the hot oil. Use tongs to fold tortillas and hold edges open. Fry, turning once or twice, until crisp and lightly browned. Drain, and remove to paper towels to complete draining. Keep taco shells warm in a 200° oven while preparing remainder.

Lightly mix lettuce and dressing. Fill each taco with tuna mixture, then top with lettuce and shredded cheese. Serve chile salsa to taste. Makes 4 servings, 2 tacos each.

Tools for Tacos

When you fry taco shells, it's a challenge to keep them from folding together—making them difficult to fill. A taco cooker is an attempt to make the process easier. This utensil has two perforated metal sleeves with a long scissors-like handle. Place the tortilla between the two sleeves and lower it into the hot oil. You can remove the tortilla after a minute or so, as soon as the fold is crisply set, then turn it with tongs to finish cooking the upper edges.

If you make several tacos at a time, you may find a taco holder handy. It holds the warm fried taco shells upright while you fill them.

The style of taco in the previous three recipes is fairly standard in the U.S., but rarely seen very far south of the Mexican border. You will still find tacos, but they take different forms. Here is a Mexico City version—the tortilla rolled around a meaty piece of boneless chicken into a tight cylinder, then crisply fried. It's served with familiar garnishes of sour cream and *guacamole* (a well-seasoned avocado dip), so that the overall taco effect is much the same. This sort of taco is similar to what is called a *flauta* in parts of the West and Southwest.

Chicken Tacos with Guacamole *(Tacos de Pollo con Guacamole)*

3 halved chicken breasts (about 1½ lbs.)
¼ cup chopped onion
½ cup water
1 teaspoon salt
¼ teaspoon *each* whole black peppers and coriander seeds
1 sprig cilantro *or* ¼ teaspoon dried cilantro
   Salt
12 corn tortillas, softened (see page 22)
   Oil for deep frying
   Sour cream, thinned with a little cream or half-and-half
   Guacamole (recipe follows)
   Sliced green onions, chopped cilantro and tomato wedges, for garnish

Place chicken breasts in a medium frying pan with onion and water. Sprinkle with salt, black peppers, coriander seeds and cilantro. Bring to boiling, cover, reduce heat and simmer until chicken is tender, 15 to 20 minutes. When chicken breasts are cool enough to handle, remove and discard skin and bones (strain and reserve broth for another use). Separate the meat into long pieces; sprinkle lightly with salt. Divide chicken among the 12 tortillas, and roll each up tightly.

Fry, one or two at a time, in deep oil heated to 350° to 375°, using tongs to hold the tacos together and keep them from unrolling during the first 30 seconds, until lightly browned and crisp. Drain on paper towels. Sprinkle with salt and place in a heatproof pan in a 250° oven to keep warm while cooking remaining tacos. Serve topped with sour cream, with guacamole at the side to spoon over each serving. Sprinkle tacos and guacamole with onions and cilantro. Garnish with tomatoes. Accompany with Refried Beans (see page 92). Makes 4 to 6 servings.

Guacamole: Halve, seed and peel 2 ripe avocados. Mash with 1 tablespoon lime juice until mixture is soft but still chunky. Lightly mix in 1/4 cup finely chopped onion, 2 tablespoons chopped fresh cilantro (*or* 2 teaspoons dried cilantro), 1/4 teaspoon salt and a dash *each* cayenne and seasoned pepper.

Crisp Cheese Tacos, Puerto Vallarta Style   *(Tacos de Queso)*

8   corn tortillas, softened (see
        page 22)
4   ounces *each* Monterey jack
        and Cheddar cheese, each cut
        in 8 2½-inch-long strips,
        ½ inch wide and ½ inch thick
Oil for deep frying
Tomato-Chile Relish (recipe fol-
        lows), *or* red or green taco
        sauce

At one side of each softened tortilla, place a strip of both Monterey jack and Cheddar cheese. Roll each cheese-filled tortilla up tightly to make a cylinder. Pour oil at least 1 inch deep into a deep heavy frying pan, electric skillet or Chinese wok; heat to 370° to 375°. Using tongs or a taco frying holder to prevent the taco from unrolling, fry, one at a time, in the hot oil until lightly browned and crisp. Drain on paper towels. Place tacos in a heatproof pan in a 250° oven to keep warm while cooking remaining tacos. Serve hot with Tomato-Chile Relish or taco sauce. Makes 4 servings, 2 tacos each.

Tomato-Chile Relish: Mix 1 small very ripe tomato, finely chopped; 2 green onions, thinly sliced (use most of the green tops); 1/4 cup chopped cilantro *or* 1 tablespoon dried cilantro, and 1 canned green chile, chopped. Cover and refrigerate for 1 hour or longer to blend flavors.

Yucatecan Soft Chicken Tacos   *(Tacos de Pollo Yucatán)*

Yet another sort of taco is a simple combination of a freshly made warm tortilla and a chicken, shellfish or meat salad. These soft chicken tacos are typical of Yucatán. They are so small—and so good, as served by a busy little taco shop in Mérida called El Cangrejito—that people order six or eight at a time.

3   cups shredded, boneless cooked
        chicken
⅓   cup mayonnaise
1   small tomato, seeded and
        chopped
2   green onions, thinly sliced (use
        part of tops)
2   tablespoons chopped fresh cilantro, *or* 1 teaspoon crumbled
        dried cilantro
Salt and pepper
24   small warm corn tortillas
        (see note)
Leaf lettuce

To prepare chicken topping, lightly mix chicken, mayonnaise, tomato, green onions, cilantro and salt and pepper to taste; cover and refrigerate for 1 to 3 hours to blend flavors. Cook tortillas on a hot griddle as directed on page 10; keep warm in a covered pan or casserole until all are cooked. Top each soft, warm tortilla with a leaf of lettuce and a dollop of chicken mixture. Serve immediately. Fold in half to eat. Makes 4 to 6 servings.

Note: Use basic Corn Tortilla recipe, page 10, dividing mixture into 24 equal portions. Press tortillas into approximately 4-1/2-inch rounds. If made ahead, reheat by sprinkling lightly with water and heating in 4 stacks, wrapped in foil, in a 300° oven for 10 to 15 minutes.

Do You Need a Deep-Fryer?

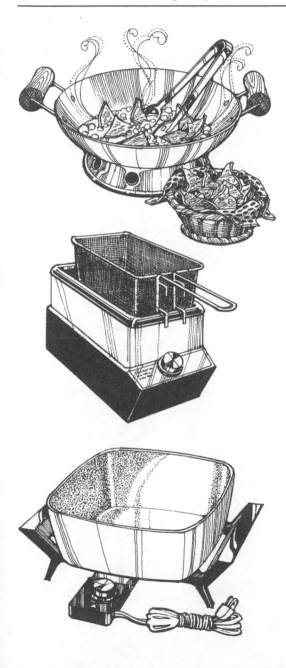

The terms "deep-frying" and "deep-fat frying" may be somewhat misleading. Both simply refer to food cooked by immersing it in hot oil or shortening. The Mexican foods cooked by this method are usually tortillas in various forms and are somewhat flat in shape. Therefore, the cooking can be accomplished in an inch or less of fat.

Tortillas, especially if they are being cooked flat, as for *tostadas*, are fairly large, so be sure you choose a utensil for deep-frying that's broad enough to accommodate them.

Deep-frying is most easily done in a thermostatically controlled container, such as an electric deep-fryer or an electric frying pan. An electric wok also works well. If you use a non-electric frying pan, a French-style *frite* pan or a wok on top of the range, it's important to use a frying thermometer, so that you can be aware of and control temperature variations. If oil overheats, foods will burn; if the temperature drops too low, they become grease-soaked. The temperature for deep frying ranges between 325° and 375°. (See each recipe for specific directions.)

For turning foods as they cook in deep fat, use long-handled tongs. An especially useful kind are bamboo tongs from the Orient, for they remain cooler to the touch than metal tongs do. You can find them in Chinese and Japanese grocery and hardware stores and in many gourmet cookware shops.

Fats for Deep-Frying

The fat most used for deep-frying (and most other purposes) in Mexican cooking is lard. Using lard for frying will give Mexican dishes a certain authenticity of flavor, but it has a lower smoking point than vegetable oils. If lard is heated to too high a temperature, it will break down and develop a poor flavor.

For repeated use, you may prefer to choose a vegetable oil such as corn, cottonseed, soybean, safflower or peanut oil. Peanut oil is often selected for high-temperature frying in Chinese and French cooking because of its high smoking point, which enables the fat to hold up better.

In any case, you will get better prolonged use from your frying fat if you take care that the frying temperature doesn't exceed that recommended in the recipe. *Never* heat any fat above 400°. After each use, allow the fat or oil to cool, then strain it through several thicknesses of dampened cheesecloth to remove food particles. Store the strained fat in a covered container in the refrigerator.

When after repeated use the fat begins to develop a strong odor (or if it bubbles and foams excessively during frying), it is time to discard and replace it. After fat is used for frying fish it should not be reused except to fry more fish.

Tostadas (say *toast*-AH-*dahs*) are similar to tacos in content, but in form they allow for greater flights of fancy, sometimes rising to astonishing heights. I think of a tostada as layer upon layer of wonderful tasting things. It begins with a tortilla fried to shattery crispness, then heaped high with warm beans, savory meat or chicken, a crunchy salad layer, shredded cheese, some avocado and colorful accents of tomatoes, radishes and green onions.

One of the most fascinating things about a tostada is the reckless way in which it combines foods that are both hot and cold. I can think of no other cuisine in which such daring chances are taken routinely—and accomplished with such seeming nonchalance!

Here are some of my favorites. The Jaliscan version, though it would be called a tostada in California, becomes a *totopo* (say *toe*-TOE-*poh*) in Mexico City and in Arizona. Because of the pickled pepper dressing, it has the hottest flavor of the three tostadas.

Super Supper Tostadas

1 small onion, chopped
1 tablespoon *each* salad oil and
    butter or margarine
1 can (1 lb.) refried beans
½ teaspoon chile powder
½ cup shredded Monterey jack
    cheese
8 corn tortillas, crisply fried
    in deep hot oil (350° to 375°)
    Ground Beef Sauce (recipe
    follows)
1 cup shredded Cheddar cheese
3 cups shredded iceberg lettuce
½ cup sour cream, thinned with
    3 tablespoons whipping
    cream or half-and-half
1 package (6 oz.) frozen avocado
    dip, thawed
    Grated Parmesan cheese, tomato
    wedges and radish roses

In a frying pan cook onion in mixture of oil and butter until soft and beginning to brown. Stir in refried beans and chile powder. Cook over medium heat, stirring occasionally, until beans are heated through. Mix in Monterey jack cheese until melted.

To serve tostadas, spread each hot crisp tortilla with bean mixture, then top with hot Ground Beef Sauce, Cheddar cheese, lettuce, a spoonful of sour cream and a dollop of avocado dip. To garnish, sprinkle with Parmesan cheese and add tomato wedges and radish roses. Makes 4 servings, 2 tostadas each.

Ground Beef Sauce: Brown 1 pound crumbled ground beef and 1 medium onion, chopped, in 1 tablespoon *each* salad oil and butter or margarine; spoon off excess fat. Mix in 1 can (8 oz.) tomato sauce, 1 teaspoon *each* garlic salt and chile powder, and 1/4 teaspoon crumbled oregano. Bring to boiling, reduce heat and simmer, covered, for 10 minutes; then uncover and continue cooking until most of the liquid is gone, stirring occasionally.

Chicken and Avocado Tostadas

3 halved chicken breasts (about
     1½ lbs.), cooked
3 cups shredded iceberg lettuce
2 green onions, thinly sliced (use
     part of tops)
4 radishes, thinly sliced
2 tablespoons chopped fresh
     cilantro or parsley
2½ tablespoons bottled
     Italian salad dressing
12 corn tortillas, crisply fried in
     deep hot oil (350° to 375°)
     Spicy Refried Beans (recipe
     follows)
2 avocados, sliced
1½ cups shredded Cheddar cheese
     Tomato wedges, carrot curls
     and radish roses, for garnish

Remove skin and bones from chicken; using your fingers, separate chicken into small shreds to make about 1 cup. Cut remainder into long strips. Mix lettuce, onions, radishes, cilantro, dressing and shredded chicken lightly. Spread hot fried tortillas with hot beans, then top with a mound of the lettuce mixture. Over lettuce place long strips of chicken breast and avocado slices. Sprinkle with cheese, using about 2 tablespoons for each. Garnish with tomato wedges, carrot curls and radish roses. Makes 4 to 6 servings.

Spicy Refried Beans: Remove casings and crumble 2 chorizo sausages (about 6 oz.) into a frying pan. Cook, stirring, until meat begins to brown; stir in 1 small onion, chopped. Cook until onion is lightly browned. Spoon off excess fat. Mix in 1 can (1 lb.) refried beans; cook until heated through. Stir in 1/2 cup shredded Monterey jack cheese until melted.

Jaliscan Chicken Totopo   *(Totopo Jalisciense con Pollo)*

1 small onion, finely chopped
1 tablespoon *each* salad oil and
     butter or margarine
1 can (1 lb.) refried beans
½ teaspoon chile powder
½ cup shredded Monterey jack cheese
4 cups shredded iceberg lettuce
2 green onions, thinly sliced
¼ cup shredded carrot
2 cups shredded, boneless
     cooked chicken
2 avocados, sliced
     Pickled Pepper Dressing
     (recipe follows)
8 corn tortillas, crisply fried in
     deep hot oil (350° to 375°)
2 small tomatoes, sliced
⅓ cup shredded Parmesan cheese

In a frying pan cook onion in mixture of oil and butter until soft and beginning to brown. Stir in refried beans and chile powder. Cook over medium heat, stirring occasionally, until beans are heated through. Mix in Monterey jack cheese until melted. In a bowl, lightly mix lettuce, green onions, carrot, chicken, one of the avocados and Pickled Pepper Dressing.

To serve totopos, spread each hot crisp tortilla with bean mixture, then mound lettuce and chicken mixture generously over the beans. Garnish with remaining sliced avocado, tomato slices and a sprinkling of Parmesan cheese. Serve immediately. Makes 4 servings.

Pickled Pepper Dressing: In blender mix 3 pickled small yellow wax peppers, stemmed and coarsely chopped; 1 tablespoon of the liquid in which they were packed; 1 teaspoon vinegar; 1/4 teaspoon *each* salt and turmeric and 1/4 cup salad oil. Whirl until smooth. Makes about 1/3 cup.

If any one dish is synonymous with Mexican cooking, it is the *enchilada* (say *ain-chee*-LAH-*dah*). Devotees of Mexican restaurants in the U.S. expect their enchiladas to take the form of a tortilla rolled around a meat, poultry or cheese filling and to be served in a generous sauce. But when one orders an enchilada in Mexico, it often takes other forms. The tortillas may well be folded or stacked to enclose the filling. Generally the tortilla in an enchilada is soft, not crisp.

When you have enchiladas in a restaurant, they're usually assembled to order, combining a hot tortilla, hot filling and a hot sauce. At home it is easier to prepare them in family-sized quantities as a baked casserole. You can get the baking dish all ready to put into the oven, then cover and refrigerate it, if you wish, and have it done hours ahead. If the enchiladas in any of the following recipes are at refrigerator temperature when you put them into the oven, allow an extra 10 to 15 minutes for them to heat through.

The tortillas in the first recipe are folded in half around a chicken, tomato and green chile filling and sprinkled with *queso fresco* (say KAY-*so* FREH-*sco*). If you can shop in a Mexican grocery store, look for this crumbly fresh white cheese. *Queso fresco* is made in small, flat round cakes and is quite perishable (use it within three or four days of purchase).

Mexico City Enchiladas *(Enchiladas Mexicanas)*

1 frying chicken (2½ to 3 lbs.), cut up
1½ teaspoons salt
¾ teaspoon ground cumin
½ teaspoon crumbled oregano
1 medium onion, finely chopped
1 small dried red pepper, crushed
1 clove garlic, minced or pressed
1 small can (4 oz.) green chiles,
 seeded and cut in long strips
1 can (1 lb.) tomatoes
1 can (8 oz.) tomato sauce
12 corn tortillas
¼ cup salad oil
½ cup crumbled Mexican-style
 queso fresco, Feta or shredded
 Monterey jack cheese
4 thin mild red onion slices,
 separated into rings

Arrange chicken pieces in a single layer in a large frying pan. Sprinkle with salt, cumin, oregano, chopped onion, crushed red pepper, garlic and green chiles. Pour on tomatoes and their liquid. Bring to boiling, reduce heat, cover and simmer for 1-1/2 hours, until chicken is very tender. Using a slotted spoon, remove chicken. When cool enough to handle, remove meat and separate it into bite-sized shreds; discard bones and skin (you should have about 3 cups meat).

Bring cooking liquid to boiling, stirring frequently, and cook until it is reduced to about 2 cups. Skim off fat, if necessary. Mix in tomato sauce. Mix 1/2 cup of the sauce with the chicken. Pour half of the remaining sauce into a shallow ungreased baking dish about 13 by 9 inches. Cook tortillas, one at a time, in heated oil in a medium frying pan until blistered and limp; drain. Fill each with about 1/4 cup of the chicken mixture. Fold in halves and arrange, slightly overlapping, in sauce in baking dish. Spoon on remaining sauce. Bake, uncovered, in a 375° oven until bubbly and heated through, 20 to 25 minutes. Sprinkle with cheese and onion rings. Makes 4 to 6 servings.

Tortillas Take a Soft Touch

Unless tortillas are fresh and warm, they are often too stiff to roll or fold without breaking. When you make tortillas to use in another dish, keep them pliable by stacking them in a foil-lined pan or dish, then cover them tightly until you're ready to use them—preferably within an hour or two.

Packaged tortillas or homemade tortillas from the refrigerator usually need to be softened before you can bend them in any way. You can do this by sprinkling them very lightly with water, then heating briefly on each side on a seasoned griddle. Heat each tortilla just long enough to soften and warm it, then stack them as if they were freshly made.

Or, use your fingertips to moisten the tortillas lightly, wrap them in foil, and heat in a 350° oven for 10 to 15 minutes, just until they are limp. You can also use a microwave oven to soften tortillas: place stacks of six in a plastic bag and allow about 45 seconds to 1 minute for up to 1 dozen.

Swiss-Style Enchiladas *(Enchiladas Suizas)*

The designation "Suizas," or Swiss-style, for enchiladas usually means that they are prepared with a good measure of dairy products such as cream and cheese. Here are two versions. The first is typically creamy and rich, and the second is also creamy but with a light, fresh tomato sauce.

2 cups shredded, boneless cooked chicken breasts
½ teaspoon salt
¼ teaspoon ground cumin
3 green onions, thinly sliced (use part of tops)
1 cup whipping cream
1 can (4 oz.) diced green chiles
¼ cup salad oil
12 corn tortillas
2 cups shredded Monterey jack cheese
½ cup grated Parmesan cheese
1 avocado, sliced

For filling, lightly mix chicken, salt, cumin and green onions. In a shallow bowl mix whipping cream and green chiles. Heat oil in a small frying pan over moderately high heat. Fry tortillas, one at a time, in heated oil until blistered and limp; drain. Dip fried tortillas in cream mixture, then fill with chicken mixture. Roll up and place, side-by-side with seam-sides down, in a greased baking dish about 13 x 9 inches. Pour on remaining cream mixture, distributing green chiles evenly. Sprinkle evenly with cheeses. Bake, uncovered, in a 375° oven for 25 to 30 minutes, until cheese is melted and lightly browned. Garnish with avocado slices. Makes 4 to 6 servings.

Swiss-Style Enchiladas II *(Enchiladas Suizas)*

1   frying chicken (2½ to 3 lbs.), cut up
2   ripe medium or large tomatoes,
         peeled and chopped
½   cup water
1   medium onion, chopped
1   clove garlic, minced or pressed
1½ teaspoons salt
¼   teaspoon *each* ground cumin
         and coriander
2   canned green chiles, chopped
1   cup whipping cream
12   corn tortillas
2   cups shredded Monterey jack
         cheese
½   cup sour cream, mixed until
         smooth with 2 tablespoons
         whipping cream or half-and-
         half
¼   cup sliced ripe olives
2   green onions, thinly sliced
         (use part of tops)

Arrange chicken pieces in a single layer in a large frying pan. Add tomatoes, water, onion, garlic, salt, cumin and coriander. Bring to boiling, cover, reduce heat and simmer for 1-1/2 hours, until chicken is very tender. Remove chicken pieces and, when chicken is cool enough to handle, remove and discard bones and skin. Use your fingers to shred chicken into bite-sized pieces (you should have about 3 cups).

Meanwhile, bring cooking liquid to boiling and boil slowly, stirring occasionally, until sauce is thickened and reduced to about 1-1/2 cups; stir in green chiles. Spread sauce in a 13 by 9-inch baking dish. Heat cream in a small frying pan. Dip tortillas, one at a time, in hot cream until limp. Fill with chicken. Roll up and place, side-by-side, in sauce in baking pan. Pour on remaining cream. Sprinkle with cheese. Bake, uncovered, in a 375° oven for 20 to 25 minutes, until filling is heated through and cheese is melted and lightly browned. Spoon sour cream down the centers of the enchiladas; sprinkle with ripe olives and green onions. Serve immediately. Makes 4 to 6 servings.

Made with canned enchilada sauce, these zesty chicken enchiladas are quick to put together.

Chicken and Green Chile Enchiladas

1 can (10 oz.) enchilada sauce
12 corn tortillas
1½ pounds chicken breasts, cooked,
    boned, skinned and cut in
    12 lengthwise pieces
1½ cups *each* shredded Cheddar and
    Monterey jack cheeses, mixed
1 can (4 oz.) diced green chiles
    Sour cream, sliced green onions
    and sliced ripe olives, for garnish

Heat enchilada sauce in a small frying pan. Soften tortillas by dipping each in warm sauce. On each tortilla, place a long piece of chicken, about 1 tablespoon of cheese mixture and 2 teaspoons chiles. Roll tortillas and place, seam-sides down, side-by-side in a greased 13 by 9-inch baking dish. Pour on remaining sauce. Sprinkle evenly with remaining cheeses. Bake, uncovered, in a 375° oven until cheese is melted and bubbly and enchiladas are heated through, 15 to 20 minutes. Spoon sour cream down the center and sprinkle it with olive and green onion slices. Makes 4 to 6 servings.

Bean and Cheese Enchiladas

Enchiladas filled with beans and topped liberally with cheese make an inexpensive main dish. You might also serve them as an accompaniment to grilled steak or hamburgers.

2 chorizo sausages (about 6 oz.)
1 recipe (see page 92) Refried Red,
    Pink or Pinto beans, prepared
    up to the point of heating in
    fat, *or* 1 can (1 lb.) refried beans
1 small onion, finely chopped
1 tablespoon salad oil
1 large can (15 oz.) tomato sauce
¼ cup water
2 canned green chiles, chopped
½ teaspoon garlic powder
1 teaspoon chile powder
12 corn tortillas
1 cup *each* shredded Cheddar and
    Monterey jack cheese
    Sliced green onions, for garnish

Remove sausage casings; crumble meat. Cook in a 9 to 10-inch frying pan over medium heat, stirring occasionally, until meat is browned; spoon off drippings. Mix in Refried Beans and cook until heated through; remove from heat.

In a medium-sized frying pan cook onion in heated oil until soft and lightly browned. Mix in tomato sauce, water, green chiles, garlic powder and chile powder. Bring to boiling, cover, reduce heat, and simmer for 10 minutes. Dip tortillas, one at a time, in hot tomato sauce until limp. Drain, then fill with Refried Beans, using about 3 tablespoons for each. Roll tortillas and place seam-side down, side-by-side in an ungreased 13 by 9-inch baking dish. Spread with remaining tomato sauce. Sprinkle evenly with cheeses. Bake, uncovered, in a 375° oven for 25 to 30 minutes, until cheese is melted and lightly browned. Sprinkle with green onions. Makes 4 to 6 servings.

Flauta (rhymes with *about-a*) is the Spanish word for flute, which this taco variation rather resembles. It is made from two tortillas, overlapped then filled and crisply fried. Cook the beef for the filling until it is so tender it can be separated easily into slender shreds.

Beef Flautas

1	pound lean beef stew meat, cut in large cubes
	Salt, pepper and chile powder
2	tablespoons lard or shortening
1	large onion, finely chopped
1	clove garlic, minced or pressed
1	cup tomato juice
16	corn tortillas, softened (see page 22)
	Oil for deep frying
	Salt
	Shredded lettuce
½	cup sour cream, mixed with 3 tablespoons whipping cream or half-and-half
1	package (6 oz.) frozen avocado dip, thawed
	Shredded Parmesan cheese
1	tomato, cut in wedges

For filling, sprinkle beef cubes with salt, pepper and chile powder. Brown on all sides in heated lard or shortening in a large frying pan. Mix in onion, garlic and tomato juice. Bring to boiling, cover, reduce heat and simmer slowly until meat is very tender, about 2-1/2 hours. Using two forks, shred beef into lengthwise fibers. Cook, uncovered, until most of the liquid is gone. (You should have about 2 cups filling). Filling can be made ahead and refrigerated.

For each flauta, overlap two tortillas down the centers. Place about 1/4 cup of the beef filling down the center, and roll tightly. In oil, at least 1-inch deep heated to 350° to 375°, fry flautas one or two at a time. Use tongs to hold the flautas together and keep them from unrolling during the first 30 seconds; fry until lightly browned and crisp. Drain on paper towels, sprinkle with salt and place in a heatproof pan in a 250° oven to keep warm while cooking remaining flautas. Serve on a bed of lettuce, topped with sour cream, then a dollop of avocado dip and a sprinkling of cheese. Garnish with tomatoes. Makes 4 servings.

Tamale making is something of a chore, as each little cornhusk-wrapped packet is prepared individually. It is easier if you can enlist two or more friends or family members to help—one to prepare the cornhusks, one to make the *masa* that encloses the filling, and another to cook the filling. When assembling the tamales use a similar division of labor.

You can wrap the tamales in fresh green cornhusks, or dried husks saved from summer sweet corn and later washed and soaked to make them pliable. Dried cornhusks are available in 8-ounce packages (enough for 75 to 100 tamales) in Mexican grocery stores.

The filling for these tamales is a mildly seasoned chicken mixture with pine nuts or almonds.

Chicken Tamales

1 frying chicken (2½ to 3 lbs.), cut up
1 large onion, finely chopped
1 clove garlic, minced or pressed
1½ teaspoons salt
1 small dried red pepper, crushed
½ cup water
1 can (8 oz.) tomato sauce
½ teaspoon *each* ground cloves and coriander
¼ cup pine nuts or slivered almonds
Prepared cornhusks (directions follow)
Masa Dough (recipe follows)

Place chicken pieces (including heart and gizzard, if you wish, but not the liver) in a large deep frying pan or Dutch oven. Add onion, garlic, salt, crushed red pepper and water. Bring to boiling, cover, reduce heat and simmer for 1-1/2 hours, until chicken is very tender. Remove chicken pieces, reserving cooking liquid. Remove and discard skin and bones. Tear or cut chicken into bite-sized pieces; finely chop heart and gizzard, if used. To cooking liquid add tomato sauce, cloves, coriander, pine nuts or almonds and chicken. Bring to boiling, reduce heat, cover and simmer for 30 minutes; uncover and continue cooking, stirring occasionally, until most of the liquid is gone and sauce is thick (you should have about 4 cups).

Arrange cornhusks, overlapping if necessary, on a flat surface with wide ends toward you. On each, spread *masa* dough thinly in about a 4 by 3-inch rectangle with one short edge at the right edge of the cornhusk. Over the *masa,* spoon about 1 scant tablespoon of the chicken filling. To fold tamales, fold the right edge of the corn husk to the center, then fold the left edge over it, so that the masa meets in the center. Fold the bottom end toward the middle, then fold the pointed end over it. Turn tamales over to hold the husks in place. (This much can be done ahead and refrigerated for up to 24 hours.)

To cook tamales, stack them, folded-sides down, in a vegetable steamer or on a rack placed well above about 2 inches of water in a deep covered kettle. Arrange tamales loosely enough so that steam can circulate. Cover steamer or kettle and place over medium heat; bring water to a gentle boil. Steam for about 45 minutes, until dough of tamales removed from the center and top is firm and no longer tastes doughy. Serve immediately. Makes 6 servings, 6 to 8 tamales each.

Masa Dough: Beat 3/4 cup lard until fluffy. Blend in 2-1/2 cups *masa harina* (packaged corn tortilla flour), 1 teaspoon salt and 1-1/2 cups warm water or chicken broth until the dough holds together well. Cover and keep dough cool until ready to use.

To prepare cornhusks: If using fresh cornhusks, dry in the sun for several days until dried and yellow; store in plastic bags. Or purchase dried cornhusks in a Mexican grocery store. Before using the husks, soak in warm water until pliable. Wash thoroughly to remove bits of silk, etc.; drain. Cover with warm water and soak for 2 hours or overnight, keeping the husks damp until used. Pat them dry before spreading with dough. If you are using fresh cornhusks, you may have to overlap two or more of them to get a large enough surface for each tamale.

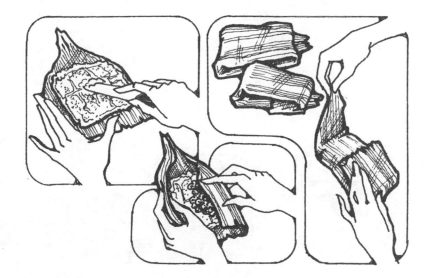

Wheat was introduced to Mexico in Colonial times, eventually giving rise to flour tortillas. They are especially popular in the state of Sonora in the northwest. A number of enjoyable Mexican dishes, notably *burritos* (say *boo*-REE-*toes*), require them. If you prefer them, they can be used in place of corn tortillas in many recipes.

Flour tortillas require more skill and persistence to make than do the corn ones. Because different flours absorb moisture at different rates, you should add the liquid gradually, assessing the consistency of the dough to be sure it is neither too wet nor too dry. Then, because of the gluten (protein) content of wheat flour, flour tortillas are too elastic to be made with a tortilla press. They must be rolled out individually.

Don't be discouraged! Once you develop a feel for them they can be made very quickly. Homemade flour tortillas are so much better than even the best packaged ones, that it is worth learning to make your own.

Pat Gonzalez' Flour Tortillas

2   cups unsifted all-purpose flour
1   teaspoon *each* salt and baking
       powder
1   tablespoon lard
       Cold water (⅔ to ¾ cup)

In the large bowl of an electric mixer, mix flour, salt and baking powder. Cut in lard until mixture is uniform. Gradually mix in water to make a soft dough that does not feel sticky to the touch. Divide dough into 9 or 12 equal portions; roll each into a small ball. Roll each out paper-thin on a well floured board or pastry cloth to a circle about 10 inches in diameter if making 9 tortillas or 8 inches in diameter if making 12. Cook tortillas on a seasoned (but ungreased) large griddle over medium heat, turning two or three times, until bubbly and lightly browned on each side. Makes 9 large or 12 medium-sized flour tortillas.

Burritos seem to taste better if they are put together shortly before serving. You can make the sauce and filling ahead, if you wish, and reheat them just before assembling burritos. For best flavor, serve burritos piping hot: a few minutes under the broiler just before serving will reheat them to a sizzling temperature. Here are three varieties: beef with tomato sauce, chicken with a tart green sauce, and pork cooked with green chiles and the tangy little Mexican green tomatoes called tomatillos (see page 88).

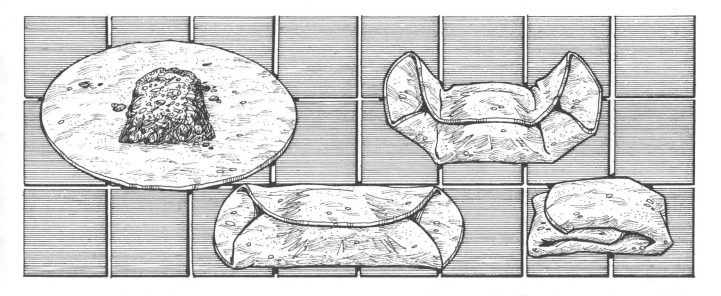

Beef Burritos with Red Sauce

1½   pounds lean beef stew meat, cut
     in large cubes
     Salt and chile powder
2   tablespoons lard or shortening
1   large onion, finely chopped
1   clove garlic, minced or pressed
1   small dried red pepper, crushed
1   teaspoon ground cumin
1   can (1 lb.) tomatoes
1   can (6 oz.) tomato paste
6   large flour tortillas (see page 28)
½   cup *each* shredded Monterey jack
     and Cheddar cheese

Sprinkle beef cubes with salt and chile powder. Brown on all sides in heated lard or shortening in a large frying pan. Spoon off excess fat. Mix in onion, garlic, red pepper, cumin, tomatoes and tomato paste. Bring to boiling, cover, reduce heat and simmer slowly until meat is very tender, about 2-1/2 hours. Remove beef; using two forks, shred beef into lengthwise fibers. Mix 1/4 cup of the sauce with beef. To remaining sauce, you can add up to 1/2 cup water to dilute to sauce-like consistency, if necessary; stir and reheat to boiling. Warm tortillas on griddle or wrapped in foil in a 325° oven until they are soft. Divide beef filling among the 6 tortillas, folding in edges and rolling up loosely. Place, side-by-side, seam-sides down in a greased baking dish. Pour on remaining sauce (reheated, if necessary). Sprinkle with cheese. Place under broiler for 2 to 3 minutes, until cheese melts. Makes 6 servings.

Chicken Burritos with Green Sauce

1 frying chicken (2½ to 3 lbs.), cut up
1 can (13 or 14 oz.) *tomatillos*
  (Mexican green tomatoes),
  quartered
1 large onion, chopped
1 clove garlic, minced or pressed
¼ cup chopped fresh cilantro, *or*
  1 tablespoon dried cilantro
1 small can (4 oz.) green chiles,
  seeded and chopped
½ teaspoon ground cumin
¼ teaspoon oregano
  Salt
6 large flour tortillas (see page 28)
1 cup shredded Monterey jack
  cheese

Place chicken pieces in a large deep frying pan or Dutch oven. Top with *tomatillos* and their liquid, onion, garlic, cilantro, green chiles, cumin and oregano. Bring to boiling, cover, reduce heat and simmer for 1-1/2 hours, or until chicken is very tender. With a slotted spoon remove chicken pieces; when cool enough to handle, remove and discard bones and skin, and separate meat into generous bite-sized pieces. Bring sauce to boiling and cook, stirring occasionally, until slightly thickened and reduced to about 2 cups; salt to taste. Reheat chicken in 1/2 cup of the sauce. Warm tortillas on a griddle, or wrap in foil and heat in a 350° oven for about 15 minutes; divide filling among the 6 tortillas, folding in edges and rolling up loosely. Place, side-by-side, seam-sides down in a greased baking dish. Pour on remaining sauce, reheated, if necessary. Sprinkle with cheese. Place under broiler just long enough to melt and lightly brown cheese. Serve at once. Makes 6 servings.

Pork and Green Chile Burritos *(Chipichangas)*

1½ pounds lean boneless pork, cut
  in 1-inch cubes
  Salt and ground cumin
1½ tablespoons lard
1 large onion, chopped
1 clove garlic, minced or pressed
1 cup chopped fresh or drained
  canned *tomatillos* (Mexican
  green tomatoes)
1 small can (4 oz.) green chiles,
  seeded and chopped
½ teaspoon crumbled oregano
2 tablespoons chopped fresh cilantro, *or* 1 teaspoon dried cilantro
½ cup water
6 large flour tortillas (see page 28)
  Shredded iceberg lettuce
½ cup sour cream, thinned with 3
  tablespoons half-and-half

1 package (6 oz.) frozen avocado
  dip, thawed
  Grated Parmesan cheese
  Tomato wedges, for garnish

Sprinkle pork with salt and cumin. Brown in heated lard in a large heavy frying pan. Spoon off excess fat, if necessary. Add onion, garlic, *tomatillos,* green chiles, oregano, cilantro and water. Bring to boiling, cover, reduce heat and simmer for about 1-1/2 hours, until meat is very tender. Uncover and simmer for 15 to 20 minutes longer, stirring occasionally, until thickened. Salt to taste. Warm tortillas on a griddle, or wrap in foil and heat in a 350° oven for 15 minutes; divide pork filling among the 6 tortillas, rolling up loosely. For each serving, place a burrito atop shredded lettuce; spoon on sour cream, then avocado dip. Sprinkle with cheese and garnish with a tomato wedge. Makes 6 servings.

APPETIZERS & DRINKS

David B. Redmond

Mealtimes in Mexico tend to be later than corresponding meals in North America. Maybe that is why visitors so quickly become acquainted with many between and before-meal foods. In this chapter are collected some favorite foods for snacking while the enchiladas bake or the soup simmers.

The all-purpose conveyor of dips and spreads is the *tostadita* (say *toast-ah-DEE-tah*), which in some areas is also called a *tostada*. Although this must be the prototype for packaged corn chips and tortilla chips, when you take the time to make your own, they are enormously better.

Homemade Corn Chips *(Tostaditas)*

Using kitchen scissors, cut tortillas into 4 or 6 pie-shaped wedges. Pour salad oil or peanut oil into a heavy frying pan, electric frying pan or Chinese wok to a depth of at least 1/2 inch; heat to a temperature of 350° to 375°. Fry corn chips, a few at a time, until crisp and lightly browned. Remove with tongs or a slotted spoon to paper towels to drain. Salt lightly.

Melted Cheese Dip *(Chile con Queso)*

A melted cheese dip called *chile con queso* (say CHEE-*leh cohn* KAY-*so*) is popular both in Mexico and in the southwestern United States.

1½ cups shredded Monterey jack
      cheese
 ½ cup shredded Cheddar cheese
 ¼ cup half-and-half (light cream)
 1 canned green chile, seeded and
      chopped
 1 small tomato,
      peeled and finely chopped

Over moderately low heat, combine cheeses and half-and-half in a saucepan or small frying pan. Heat, stirring frequently, until melted and smooth. Mix in chopped green chile and tomato. Transfer to a heatproof container on a warming tray or over a candle warmer. Scoop up warm cheese dip with *tostaditas* or packaged corn chips. Makes 1-1/2 cups.

All About Avocados

At different times of the year, you'll find two varieties of California avocados in your market. In summer one sees more of the dark bumpy-skinned Hass avocado; and in winter the lighter green, thinner-skinned Fuerte avocado is more plentiful. Florida avocados resemble the Fuerte, but are larger and contain somewhat less oil.

Make sure the avocado is ripe; usually they are firm when you buy them. Everyone has a favorite method for achieving just the right consistency. One that many people recommend is to place the avocado in a paper bag at room temperature until it just yields to gentle pressure when held in the palm of the hand (poking an avocado may bruise it) and squeezed lightly. Then you can transfer the avocado to the refrigerator until you are ready for it. It is best if used within two or three days after ripening.

To peel and pit a ripe avocado, cut it lengthwise around the middle, cutting all the way to the seed. Separate the halves by turning them in opposite directions. To remove the seed, give it a brisk blow with the blade of a sharp knife. Hit it hard enough so the knife is impaled in the seed. Then twist the knife and lift out the seed. Peel off skin with a paring knife.

Mexican Avocado Dip *(Guacamole)*

With homemade corn chips, nothing is better than *guacamole* (say *gwah-kah-MOE-leh*). Some people make this savory avocado dip in a blender, but it is vastly more appealing if you mash the mixture with a fork, leaving the avocados somewhat chunky. Guacamole is also good as a dip for crisp fresh vegetables, or served as a salad atop shredded lettuce and cherry tomatoes.

3 avocados, halved, seeded and
    peeled
    Juice of 1 lime
½ cup finely chopped mild red
    onion, *or* ¼ cup thinly sliced
    green onions
¼ cup chopped fresh cilantro, *or*
    1 tablespoon dried cilantro
⅛ teaspoon cayenne or
    Tabasco sauce
½ teaspoon salt
    Dash seasoned pepper

Mash avocados with lime juice until soft but still a little chunky. Lightly mix in remaining ingredients. Sprinkle with additional chopped onions and fresh cilantro, if you wish. Serve with *tostaditas* (see page 32), corn chips or warm corn tortillas as a dip. For guacamole salad, serve a dollop of the avocado mixture atop individual servings of shredded lettuce, garnished with halved cherry tomatoes. Makes about 2 cups.

When you consider how much of the tuna we consume is caught off the west coast of Mexico, it is not surprising that tuna should be popular in Mexico, too. This is a nice dip for a party or buffet, and it also makes a good sandwich spread.

Tropical Tuna Dip   *(Antojito de Atun)*

1   can (6½ oz.) chunk light tuna,
     drained and flaked
2   green onions, thinly sliced (use
     part of tops)
1   canned green chile, seeded and
     chopped
1   tablespoon lime or lemon juice
     Dash Tabasco sauce
¼   cup mayonnaise
     Tostaditas (see page 32) or
     packaged corn chips

Lightly mix tuna, green onions, green chile, lime or lemon juice and Tabasco sauce. Fold in mayonnaise. Cover and chill for 2 to 3 hours to blend flavors. Serve as a dip for *tostaditas* or corn chips. Makes about 1-1/4 cups.

Giant Tostadas Casa Mexicana   *(Tostadas con Aceite)*

Here is another sort of tostada—a crisp oversized tortilla that is baked, flavored with cheese and hot sauce. It is served as a hot appetizer with cocktails at Casa Mexicana, a charming patio restaurant in Oaxaca.

2   cups *masa harina* (packaged corn
     tortilla flour)
1   cup warm water
     Flour
2   tablespoons melted lard (see note)
½   cup *each* shredded sharp Cheddar
     and Monterey jack cheese
     Hot red or green taco sauce or
     salsa

Mix *masa harina* and warm water in a bowl, stirring until the mixture is well blended and pulls away from sides of the bowl. With your hands, shape it into a ball, then divide into 6 equal pieces.

Dust each ball of dough with flour. Roll each out between sheets of waxed paper to a 9 to 10-inch circle; peel off waxed paper and transfer to greased or Teflon-coated baking sheets. Brush with melted lard. Bake in a 375° oven until well browned and crisp, about 15 minutes. Sprinkle each tostada with some of the cheese mixture, then drizzle with hot sauce to taste. Serve immediately. Break apart with your fingers and eat in irregular pieces. Makes 6 large appetizers.

Note: In place of lard, you may use rendered pork fat, made by cooking fatty trimmings in a frying pan until crisp and browned. Strain and use drippings.

Hot tortillas filled with cheese are called *quesadillas* (say *kay-sah*-DEE-*yahs*) and take many forms. They can be heated on a griddle, baked or fried, using corn or flour tortillas. These are made with flour tortillas and fried to puffy plumpness. At Las Cazuelas, a popular restaurant serving traditional Mexican food in the oldest section of Mexico City, a similar but smaller quesadilla accompanies the guacamole.

Cheese Filled Flour Tortillas   *(Quesadillas)*

2 cups unsifted all-purpose flour
1 teaspoon *each* salt and baking
   powder
1 tablespoon lard
⅔ to ¾ cup cold water
1½ cups *each* shredded Monterey
   jack and Cheddar cheese
1 canned green chile, seeded and
   chopped
   Oil for deep frying

In the large bowl of an electric mixer, mix flour, salt and baking powder. Cut in lard until mixture is uniform. Gradually mix in water to make a soft dough that does not feel sticky to the touch. Divide dough into 16 equal portions; roll each into a small ball. Roll each out on a well floured board or pastry cloth to a circle about 6 inches in diameter.

Mix cheeses and chile. On each tortilla, place about 3 tablespoons of the cheese mixture. Fold filled tortillas in halves to form half-moon shapes, moistening edges to seal. In a heavy frying pan, electric skillet or Chinese wok pour oil to a depth of at least 1 inch; heat to 370°. Cook quesadillas, 2 or 3 at a time, until puffy and golden brown on both sides, turning carefully, about 2-1/2 minutes total. Remove with a skimmer or slotted spoon, and drain on paper towels. Serve hot. Makes 16.

Garlic Roasted Peanuts

One of my favorite memories of Oaxaca is of munching warm, startlingly garlicky peanuts with a tart Margarita in a whitewashed courtyard. I couldn't wait to get home to see if anything as seemingly simple could be done in my own kitchen. It can! All it takes is a lot of garlic and raw peanuts. The peanuts can be found in natural food stores and in grocery stores that sell such items as lentils and dried beans in bulk. I've tried this with several kinds of peanuts, and they were all good. Somehow I think the ones with red skins taste best, perhaps because they *look* like those I first tasted in Oaxaca.

Peel and split 6 cloves garlic. Combine with 1 pound raw Spanish or redskin peanuts (with skins) and 2 teaspoons peanut oil in an 8-inch-square baking pan. Roast in a 300° oven, stirring occasionally, until peanuts are well browned, 1 hour and 20 to 30 minutes. Salt to taste. Cool; store in a covered container. Makes about 3 cups.

When you look at a display of Mexican fruits in a market or on a street vendor's cart, it is suddenly apparent that much of the country is decidedly tropical. There are mangoes, papayas, bananas, pineapples, every sort of citrus and many fruits mysterious to North American eyes.

Many of these glorious fresh fruits are blended in *jugo de siete frutas*, a popular Mexico City drink. Here is my attempt to approximate this thick, pink, exotic-tasting blend. A big glass of it is a filling breakfast all by itself, and it is also a refreshing non-alcoholic cocktail to sip before a Mexican meal.

Seven Fruits Cooler   *(Jugo de Siete Frutas)*

1   basket (about 2½ cups) ripe red
      strawberries, rinsed and
      stemmed
1   cup chopped fresh pineapple
1   mango, peeled and chopped
      (see note)
    Juice of 1 orange
    Juice of 1 grapefruit
    Juice of 1 lemon
    Juice of 1 lime
    Sugar (1 to 3 tablespoons)
    Lime slices, for garnish

In blender container place strawberries, pineapple, mango and orange juice. Whirl until mixture is smooth and liquid. Mix in grapefruit, lemon and lime juice. Sweeten with sugar to taste, if needed. Chill to blend flavors. Stir well and serve with straws in tall glasses garnished with lime slices. Makes 4 to 6 servings (about 5 cups).

Note: If you are unable to get a mango, substitute a peeled, chopped peach or nectarine, or—for a different flavor blend—1 cup chopped seeded watermelon.

Ole for Two Labor-Savers!

Once upon a time, no Mexican household could function without a *metate,* a stone mortar used for grinding corn and many other foods.

Today both the food processor and the electric blender have taken over many of the *metate's* jobs: grinding spices, herbs, seeds and nuts to powdery fineness; making smoothly combined salad dressings and marinades; and mixing batter for crêpes. As you prepare the recipes in this book, you'll find your food processor or blender a big help in performing all these tasks.

The combination of red wine and tart citrus juices makes *sangria* (say *sahn*-GREE-*ah*) a popular summer drink. These two versions are similar—the first is made with frozen limeade concentrate for spur-of-the-moment occasions. The second uses a sugar and lime juice syrup that must be prepared ahead.

Lazy Gringo Sangria

1 can (6 oz.) frozen limeade
    concentrate, thawed
1 bottle (1 fifth) dry red wine,
    chilled
Lime or lemon slices, for garnish
Club soda (optional)

Pour limeade concentrate into a 5 to 6-cup pitcher. Pour in wine. Float lime or lemon slices in the wine. To serve, stir well to combine, then pour over ice cubes in tall glasses. Add club soda to taste, if you wish. Makes 5 to 6 servings.

Red Wine and Citrus Punch *(Sangría)*

½ cup *each* sugar and water
Juice of 2 limes (about ⅓ cup)
1 bottle (1 fifth) dry red wine,
    chilled
1 *each* lime and orange, thinly
    sliced
Club soda (optional)

In a small saucepan combine sugar and water. Bring to a full rolling boil, stirring to dissolve sugar. Boil for 2 minutes. Remove from heat, and let stand until syrup is cool; stir in lime juice. Place syrup in a 5 to 6-cup pitcher. Pour in wine. Add lime and orange slices. To serve, stir well to combine, then pour over ice cubes in tall glasses. Add club soda to taste, if you wish. Makes 4 to 6 servings.

Planter's Punch

A tall frosty glass of planter's punch always recalls memories of sunsets in Puerto Vallarta or the oasis-like pool at the luxuriant Hacienda Uxmal. You may have to shop in a Mexican grocery store or a shop that features imported gourmet groceries to find guava nectar. In California many supermarkets have the refrigerated guava juice drink in one-quart bottles in the produce section.

1 cup canned guava nectar or
    bottled guava juice drink
½ cup dark rum
2 tablespoons frozen limeade
    concentrate, thawed
Dash nutmeg
Lime slices

Place ice cubes in each of two tall glasses. For each drink, pour on 1/2 cup guava nectar or guava juice drink, 1/4 cup rum, 1 tablespoon limeade concentrate and a few grains of nutmeg. Stir well. Serve garnished with lime slices; sip with straws. Makes 2 tall drinks.

Tequila has an entirely different flavor from other clear liquors such as gin and vodka, yet it shares their ability to combine with a variety of fruits and other refreshing flavors. A good example is this tall frothy drink, made with coconut juice, egg whites and lime juice. It is pleasant for a brunch with fresh fruit and one of the egg dishes in chapter four.

Tequila and Coconut Fizz

1   can (7¾ oz.) chilled sweetened
    coconut juice
½   cup tequila
3   tablespoons fine granulated sugar
2   egg whites (¼ cup)
1   teaspoon orange flower water
6   ice cubes, crushed
    Juice of 2 small limes (about
      ¼ cup)

In blender container combine coconut juice, tequila, sugar, egg whites and orange flower water. Add ice cubes and lime juice. Blend at high speed until foamy. Makes 4 drinks.

Margarita

And here is a classic Margarita for that quart of tequila you brought back from your trip to Mexico.

    Kosher or coarse salt
½   cup (4 oz.) tequila
2   tablespoons (1 oz.) orange
    liqueur, such as Grand
    Marnier, Triple Sec or
    Curaçao
    Juice of 2 limes (about ¼ cup)
1   tablespoon sugar
    Crushed ice

To prepare glasses, moisten rims, then dip into salt in a shallow dish. Let stand a few minutes to set. In a cocktail shaker or blender combine tequila, orange liqueur, lime juice and sugar. Shake or blend well until frothy. Pour into prepared glasses over crushed ice. Makes 2 drinks.

Chocolate is one of the flavors Mexico gave to the rest of the world. Spiced hot chocolate is one of the best ways of appreciating it.

Hot Chocolate with Spices, Mexicana

1 ounce (1 square) unsweetened
    chocolate
1 tablespoon honey
2 cups milk
    Pinch salt
2 cinnamon sticks, broken in
    1-inch lengths
¼ teaspoon whole cloves
    Few drops vanilla

In a 1 to 1-1/2-quart saucepan, heat chocolate and honey, stirring occasionally over low heat until chocolate melts. Gradually pour in milk, mixing until well blended. Add salt, cinnamon sticks and cloves. Heat slowly to just below the boiling point. Strain into a heatproof pitcher. Add vanilla. Beat with a wire whisk or a wooden *molinillo* (see below) until frothy. Serve immediately. Makes 2 servings.

Can You Beat That!

The curious looking wooden instrument called a *molinillo* (say *mo-lee*-NEE-*yoh*) represents one of those coincidences of art and function that goes back to antiquity. Carved from a single piece of wood, the spinning rings and tapering shape of this delightful looking utensil are designed to whip hot chocolate into a steaming froth. And it works! Hold the beater firmly between the palms of your hands in a pitcher of hot chocolate, spin it rapidly back and forth and watch the bubbles form.

So many wonderfully Mexican flavors combine in this after-dinner coffee. It tastes so good it can double as both coffee and dessert.

Mexican Spiced Coffee   *(Café Mexicano en Olla)*

6	tablespoons full-bodied dark roast coffee
	3-inch cinnamon stick, broken in several pieces
1	teaspoon Ghirardelli ground chocolate and cocoa
1	quart water

In filter paper of a drip coffee maker (such as Chemex, Melitta or other cone-style coffee maker) combine coffee, cinnamon stick and ground chocolate and cocoa. Bring water to boiling. Pour into filter in 2 or 3 additions, according to coffee maker directions. As soon as all the water has dripped through, pour the hot coffee into small round-bottomed Mexican coffee cups or other after-dinner coffee cups. Makes 4 servings, 1 cup each.

A Distinctive Mexican Clay Pot

One of the most traditional pots to be found in a Mexican market is the shiny brown pottery *olla* (say OH-*yah*). Fat and round, usually with two handles, the larger sizes are used for soups and beans. You can also find a miniature size that is just right for individual cups of coffee or hot chocolate—which is how many Mexican restaurants serve these beverages for a special touch.

FIRST COURSES, SOUPS & SALADS

David B. Redmond

The beginning of a meal in Mexico offers a delicious preview of the best and freshest foods of the area—its fruits, seafood, vegetables and local cheeses. The first courses, soups and salads in this chapter will bring this delicious diversity right to your table.

In Mexico where the fruit is lushly ripe and bursting with flavor, one can be confident that when a fruit cup is offered as a first course, it will be as boldly accented as the rest of the meal. Try fresh pineapple marinated in tequila and lime for an unforgettable combination.

Fresh Pineapple in Tequila   *(Suprema de Piña al Tequila)*

1   small to medium-sized fresh
     pineapple
½   cup tequila
     Dash salt
     Juice of 1 lime

Peel and core pineapple. Cut it into small bite-sized pieces (you should have 4 to 5 cups). Place in a glass bowl. Add tequila, salt and lime juice; mix lightly. Cover and chill for 1 to 4 hours. Serve in footed cocktail or sherbet dishes with juices spooned over. Garnish, if you wish, with a slice of lime. Makes 6 to 8 servings.

Maybe You Need a Pineapple Knife

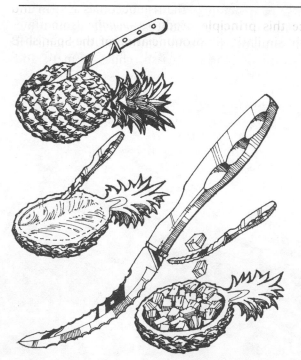

When I was a child, it was always a special day when my father brought home a fresh pineapple, for the aroma and flavor were so much more heady and exciting than those of pineapple in a can. But extracting the fruit from its armorlike skin and prickly leaves seemed an interminable struggle.

A pineapple knife can make the process much faster and easier. This knife has a long, curved serrated blade. In principle the design is similar to that of a grapefruit knife, but the blade is longer and does a cleaner job of slipping between and separating the skin from the fruit.

To cut a pineapple, use a sharp, heavy kitchen knife to cut off the crown first (omit this step if you wish to serve the pineapple from a half or quarter shell). Cut the pineapple in half lengthwise, then into quarters. Now switch to the pineapple knife. Insert the blade between the skin and the fruit and cut away the shell. Finally, use the tip of the pineapple knife to cut out any remaining bits of peel, and to cut out the core. Slice or dice the fruit into bite-sized pieces with a standard knife.

Beehives dot the Mexican landscape, and honey is much used as a natural sweetener. With lime juice, it makes a delightful syrup for a combination of fresh watermelon, papaya, pineapple and coconut.

Fresh Fruit with Coconut   *(Suprema de Frutas con Coco Fresco)*

2 tablespoons honey
   Juice of 1 lime or lemon
2 cups diced seeded watermelon
1 ripe papaya, peeled, seeded
      and diced (about 2 cups)
2 cups diced fresh pineapple
½ cup shredded fresh coconut
      (see page 117)

Mix honey and lime juice until well combined. In a serving bowl lightly mix watermelon, papaya and pineapple. Drizzle with honey mixture; mix lightly. Cover and chill for 1 to 3 hours to blend flavors. To serve, sprinkle with coconut. Makes 6 to 8 servings.

Marinated Sea Bass and Avocado   *(Ceviche)*

Marinating fish in lime juice produces an effect very similar to poaching—the fish becomes as firm and opaque as if it had been cooked using heat. In practice this principle produces *ceviche* (sometimes spelled *cebiche*, pronounced *seh-VEE-cheh*, with the slight similarity in pronunciation of the Spanish B and V). However you say it, you will find this combination of marinated fish, chiles, tomato and avocado a refreshing one.

1 pound sea bass fillet, cut in
      ½-inch cubes
   Juice of 2 limes
   Lemon juice
2 small green Serrano chiles, seeded
      and finely chopped, *or* ¼ cup
      chopped canned green chiles
¼ cup finely chopped onion
1 medium tomato, peeled and
      chopped
½ teaspoon salt
⅛ teaspoon crumbled oregano
1 tablespoon olive oil
2 tablespoons chopped fresh
      cilantro, *or* 1 teaspoon
      crumbled dried cilantro
1 avocado, peeled and diced
   Lime wedges, for garnish

Place fish in a glass bowl. Measure lime juice, and add lemon juice, if needed, to make 1/3 cup. Add to fish and mix lightly. Cover and refrigerate for several hours or overnight, until fish is white and opaque; stir occasionally. About 2 hours before serving, mix in remaining ingredients except avocado; cover again and refrigerate. To serve, mix in avocado. Serve in seafood cocktail dishes, garnished with lime wedges. Makes 4 to 6 servings.

Seafood cocktails in Mexico have an irresistible freshness and zest. One of the best combines oysters and tiny shrimp; it is typical of Campeche, on the Gulf Coast between Veracruz and the tip of Yucatán. You can make it with fresh bite-sized oysters from the Gulf of Mexico or the Eastern seaboard, or Olympia oysters from the Northwest.

Shrimp and Oyster Cocktail *(Cóctel de Campeche)*

1   can or jar (8 oz.) *fresh* shucked
     small Eastern, Gulf or Olympia
     oysters
½ pound tiny peeled cooked shrimp
1   ripe tomato, chopped
1   small green Serrano chile, seeded
     and finely chopped, *or* 2
     tablespoons chopped canned
     green chiles
2   tablespoons chopped fresh
     cilantro, *or* 1½ teaspoons dried
     cilantro
¼ cup *each* catsup and finely
     chopped onion
     Juice of 1 lime (about 1½
     tablespoons)
½ teaspoon salt
     Lime slices, for garnish

Lightly mix oysters and their liquid, shrimp, tomato, chile, cilantro, catsup, onion, lime juice and salt. Cover and chill to blend flavors for 2 to 3 hours. Serve in seafood cocktail dishes, garnished with lime slices. Makes 4 to 6 first course servings (about 3 cups).

A Knife for the Impenetrable Oyster

When you buy fresh oysters in the shells, they should be very tightly closed (if the shell is open and does not close when touched, the oyster is dead and should not be eaten). The shells are so hard that they can defy the efforts of an ordinary kitchen knife to open them.

An oyster knife is designed for the job with a short sturdy blade and a stout handle that you can wrap your fist around. When you work with oysters in the shell, it is a good idea to protect your hands from cuts and scrapes with rubber gloves or clean, heavy garden gloves.

To open an oyster, first scrub it well under cold running water to remove sand and loose pieces of shell. Then place the oyster on a board with the flatter side up. Force the blade of the oyster knife between the top and bottom shells at some point along the curved end (opposite the hinged end) of the shell. When you have pried the shells open enough, insert the knife blade between them and follow the contour of the bottom shell until you cut the adductor muscle that holds the shell closed. Pull off the top shell, cut the oyster free and serve it from the bottom shell.

Herb-Baked Fresh Oysters *(Ostiones Cardenas)*

Baked on the half shell with a garlicky herb butter, these oysters are delicious with French rolls or bread to dip into the juices.

⅓ cup soft butter
2 small green onions, thinly sliced
     (use part of tops)
2 cloves garlic, minced or pressed
¼ cup finely chopped cilantro, *or*
     1 tablespoon crumbled dried
     cilantro
¼ teaspoon salt
⅛ teaspoon *each* white pepper and
     crumbled oregano
     Dash cayenne
12 fresh oysters on the half shell

Mix butter, green onions, garlic, cilantro, salt, white pepper, oregano and cayenne. Arrange 6 oysters in shells in each of two shallow individual baking pans. Top each with a dollop of butter mixture. Bake in a 450° oven for about 6 to 8 minutes, until butter is hot and bubbling. Serve immediately, accompanied by *bolillos* (see page 100) or French bread to dip into the melted butter. Makes 2 servings.

The cold vegetable soup called *gazpacho* (say *gahs*-PAH-*cho*) is really Spanish, but it's popular in Mexico because it makes such a splendid showcase for the perfectly ripe vegetables grown in Mexican gardens. Be sure to serve it very cold. This recipe makes a larger quantity than many food processors or blenders can accommodate. Unless your food processor or blender has a 5-cup or larger container, divide the ingredients into two batches. It's not necessary to peel the tomatoes.

Blender Gazpacho

1   medium-sized cucumber
6   medium-sized very ripe tomatoes,
    coarsely chopped
¼   cup tomato paste
1   small onion, chopped
1½   cups regular-strength chicken
    broth, canned or homemade
2½   tablespoons lime or lemon juice
2   tablespoons olive oil
1½   teaspoons salt
    Dash seasoned pepper
½   teaspoon *each* sugar and
    crumbled oregano
    Condiments:
      Lime wedges, crumbled crisp
      bacon, sliced green onion,
      chopped avocado, chopped
      green chiles or green bell
      pepper, and/or coarsely
      chopped fresh cilantro or
      parsley
    Sour cream

Cut cucumber in half. Chop one half and set aside to add at the table. Peel remaining half, remove and discard seeds, and chop coarsely. In blender or food processor container combine chopped peeled cucumber, tomatoes, tomato paste, onion, broth, lime or lemon juice, olive oil, salt, pepper, sugar and oregano. Whirl until smooth and well blended. Strain soup into a bowl, cover and chill thoroughly, for up to 6 hours. To serve, stir well to blend, then ladle the cold soup into chilled bowls. Offer chopped cucumber and several of the suggested condiments and sour cream to add at the table to taste. Makes 4 to 6 servings.

Ground walnuts, whirled to a fine powder in a food processor or blender, thicken and flavor this first course soup, as well as adding a distinctive color. It is especially good if you use rich homemade chicken broth.

Creamy Walnut Soup   *(Sopa de Nuez)*

3   tablespoons butter
1   tablespoon salad oil
1   medium onion, finely chopped
¾   cup broken walnuts, whirled in
    blender or food processor
    (a few at a time) until fine
3   cups regular-strength chicken
    broth, homemade or canned
    Dash cayenne
¼   teaspoon crumbled oregano
½   cup whipping cream
    Salt and pepper

Heat butter and oil in a heavy 2 to 3-quart saucepan. In it cook onions and walnuts, stirring frequently, until onions are soft and walnuts are lightly browned. Stir in chicken broth, cayenne and oregano. Bring to boiling, reduce heat, cover and simmer for 30 minutes. Add cream and cook at a gentle boil, uncovered, for 10 minutes. Stir to mix well. Season with salt and pepper to taste. Makes 4 to 6 first course servings.

Shrimp Consomme   *(Consomé de Camarones)*

Serve this piquant shrimp soup with iced cucumber sticks for a pleasing contrast of hot and cool flavors. The broth is enriched with fish scraps and trimmings, which you may have to ask for in a market that sells fresh fish. Sometimes these odd bits, which are so essential to making a full flavored broth, are sold as "chowder fish."

1   pound fresh small shrimp in shells
2   tablespoons salad oil
1   stalk celery, finely chopped
1   large onion, thinly sliced
3   cloves garlic, minced or pressed
1   pound fish scraps and trimmings
1   can (1 lb.) tomatoes
    Small dried red peppers (2 to 3
    to taste), crushed
3   sprigs fresh cilantro, *or*
    ¼ teaspoon dried cilantro
    Juice of 1 orange (⅓ cup or more)
1   quart water
    Salt
    Lime wedges

Shell and devein shrimp, reserving shells. In heated oil in a 3 to 4-quart saucepan sauté celery, onion and garlic until soft but not browned. Add shrimp shells, fish trimmings, tomatoes (coarsely chopped) and their liquid, red peppers, cilantro, orange juice and water. Bring to boiling, cover and simmer for 1 hour. Strain, discarding solids. (This much can be done ahead, covered and refrigerated.) Add shrimp and simmer until soup is piping hot and shrimp are pink and tender, 8 to 10 minutes. Add salt to taste. Serve with lime wedges to squeeze into broth. Makes 6 first course servings.

The wonderful oysters of Mexico's extensive coastlines lend themselves to all sorts of seafood soups. Here are two quite different treatments. The first is mild, rich and creamy; the second is livelier, with tomato juice, chiles and garlic.

Creamy Oyster Soup   *(Sopa de Ostiones)*

1   medium onion, finely chopped
¼   cup finely chopped celery
2   tablespoons butter or margarine
1   can (13¾ oz.) regular-strength chicken broth
½   teaspoon salt
     Dash *each* white pepper and cayenne
2   tablespoons chopped fresh cilantro, *or* 1 teaspoon crumbled dried cilantro
1   pint (2 cups) half-and-half (light cream)
1   can or jar (8 oz.) *fresh* shucked small Eastern, Gulf or Olympia oysters

In a 2 to 3-quart saucepan sauté onion and celery in heated butter, stirring occasionally, until soft but not browned. Mix in chicken broth and seasonings. Bring to boiling, cover, reduce heat and simmer for 15 minutes. Add half-and-half, oysters and their liquid. Heat, uncovered, stirring occasionally to *just under* the boiling point (do *not* boil). Season to taste with salt and pepper. Makes 4 to 5 servings.

Spicy Tomato-Oyster Soup   *(Sopa de Ostiones y Jitomates)*

1   medium onion, finely chopped
1   tablespoon olive oil
2   cloves garlic, minced or pressed
1   can (13¾ oz.) regular-strength chicken broth
1   can (18 oz.) tomato juice
1   canned green chile, cut in thin strips
¼   cup chopped fresh cilantro, *or* 2 teaspoons dried cilantro
1   small dried red pepper, crushed
1   can or jar (8 oz.) *fresh* shucked small Eastern, Gulf or Olympia oysters, *or* 1 can (8 oz.) whole cooked oysters
     Salt
     Lime wedges

In a 2 to 3-quart saucepan, sauté onion in heated oil until tender but not browned. Mix in garlic, chicken broth, tomato juice, green chile, cilantro and dried red chile. Bring to boiling, cover, reduce heat and simmer for 30 minutes. Add oysters and their liquid; cook, uncovered, just long enough to heat oysters through, 3 to 5 minutes. Taste and add salt, if needed. Serve with lime wedges to squeeze into each bowl. Makes 4 to 5 servings.

Another soup of Spanish origin is this garlic flavored tomato broth. The soup becomes quite substantial with the addition of eggs, which are poached in it. With a salad, it is a pleasant light lunch or supper.

Spanish Garlic Soup *(Sopa de Ajo a la Española)*

10	cloves garlic, cut in quarters
2	tablespoons olive oil
1	can (18 oz.) tomato juice
1	can (13¾ oz.) regular-strength beef broth
1	bay leaf
4	eggs
	Hot tostaditas or toasted, buttered French bread

Sauté garlic in heated oil in a 2 to 3-quart saucepan until lightly browned. Add tomato juice, beef broth and bay leaf. Bring to boiling, cover, reduce heat and simmer for 15 minutes. Strain out garlic and bay leaf, reserving broth. Return broth to pan and heat to simmering. Break eggs, one at a time, into a saucer; carefully slip each into the hot broth. Poach eggs for 3 to 4 minutes, or until whites are set and yolks are still runny. Spoon eggs into 4 soup bowls; ladle broth over them. Serve with *tostaditas* or hot French bread toast. Makes 4 servings.

Tortilla Soup *(Sopa de Tortilla)*

One of the most typical of Mexican soups is this combination of a sturdy tomato purée and crisply fried tortillas. In some versions the tomato soup is so thick it seems almost a sauce, but this is somewhat lighter than that.

1	tablespoon lard
1	large onion, finely chopped
1	clove garlic, minced or pressed
1	large can (28 oz.) tomatoes
1	can (13¾ oz.) regular-strength beef broth
1	small dried red pepper, crushed
½	teaspoon *each* sugar, crumbled oregano and marjoram
⅛	teaspoon ground allspice
	Oil for deep frying
6	corn tortillas, cut in strips ½ inch wide and 2 inches long
	Salt
	Shredded Monterey jack cheese

In a 3-quart saucepan, heat lard; in it cook onion and garlic until soft but not browned. Add tomatoes (breaking them up with a fork), beef broth, crushed red pepper, sugar, oregano, marjoram and allspice. Bring to boiling, cover, reduce heat, and simmer for 1 hour. Transfer the soup, about one-third at a time, to a blender; whirl until smooth. When all the soup has been puréed, return it to pan (this much can be done ahead and reheated, if you wish). Pour oil to a depth of at least 1 inch in a heavy frying pan, electric skillet or Chinese wok; heat to 370°. Fry tortillas, a few at a time, until crisp and lightly browned; remove with skimmer or a slotted spoon and drain on paper towels. Keep warm in a 250° oven. Salt lightly. Reheat soup to serving temperature; taste and add salt, if needed. To serve, place one-fourth of the warm tortilla strips in each of 4 soup bowls. Ladle on steaming hot soup. Top each serving with a sprinkling of cheese. Serve immediately. Makes 4 servings.

The chicken and lime soup of Yucatán is one of that unique area's most appealing dishes. The rich broth should be dense with pieces of boneless chicken and so hot it *sizzles* when the crisp warm tortilla triangles are added.

Yucatecan Chicken and Lime Soup　*(Sopa de Lima)*

1　frying or stewing chicken,
　　　(3½ to 4 lbs.), cut up
1　quart water
1　large onion, coarsely chopped
1　large carrot, sliced
1　stalk celery, chopped (including
　　　leaves)
1　teaspoon salt
1　small dried red pepper, crushed
¼　teaspoon crumbled oregano
　　Juice of 2 small or 1 large lime
　　　(about 3 tablespoons)
1　large ripe tomato, peeled, seeded
　　　and chopped
　　Hot tostaditas (see page 32)
　　Thin lime slices

Place chicken in a deep 5-1/2 to 6-quart kettle or Dutch oven (if you wish, include heart and gizzard). Add water, onion, carrot, celery, salt, dried red pepper and oregano. Bring to boiling, cover and simmer slowly for about 3 hours, until broth is flavorful. Strain soup, reserving broth. Discard vegetables and seasonings. Remove and discard chicken bones and skin. Shred chicken into generous bite-sized pieces; chop giblets finely, if used. Return meat to the broth (at this point, you can cover and refrigerate soup, if made ahead). To serve, reheat soup to the boiling point; stir in lime juice and tomato. Taste and add salt, if needed. To serve, ladle soup into bowls and top each with 3 or 4 hot *tostaditas* and a lime slice. Makes 6 servings (2 to 2-1/2 quarts).

Hot Tostada Salad　*(Tostada Compuesta)*

The tostada you encountered earlier as a main dish can also be a spectacular salad that takes advantage of the tantalizing contrasts of hot and cold.

3　tablespoons salad oil
1　tablespoon cider vinegar
2　tablespoons red *salsa picante*
1　clove garlic, minced or pressed
¼　teaspoon salt
4　corn tortillas, crisply fried in
　　　deep hot oil (370° to 375°)
1　can (1 lb.) refried beans, heated
4　cups very finely shredded iceberg
　　　lettuce, chilled
½　cup shredded Cheddar cheese
4　ripe olives

For dressing, shake together (or whirl in blender) salad oil, vinegar, *salsa picante*, garlic and salt. To serve, spread hot tortillas with refried beans and place on individual heatproof plates in a 350° oven for 5 to 10 minutes, until plates, tortillas and beans are very hot. Mix chilled lettuce lightly with dressing. For each serving, heap one-fourth of the cold lettuce mixture atop each of the four prepared tortillas and, working quickly, sprinkle with cheese; garnish with olives. Serve immediately, steaming hot. Makes 4 servings.

Combining the best qualities of both a shrimp cocktail and a salad is this stuffed avocado with a lime and garlic flavored vinaigrette dressing.

Shrimp-Stuffed Avocado Salad *(Aguacate Relleno con Camarones)*

¼ cup olive oil
1½ tablespoons white wine vinegar
1 tablespoon lime or lemon juice
½ teaspoon dried cilantro
¼ teaspoon *each* salt and dry
    mustard
    Dash *each* cayenne and seasoned
    pepper
1 clove garlic, minced or pressed
½ pound tiny peeled cooked shrimp
2 large avocados
    Lime or lemon juice
    Shredded lettuce
    Halved cherry tomatoes

In a covered jar or small blender container mix oil, vinegar, the 1 tablespoon lime or lemon juice, cilantro, salt, mustard, cayenne, seasoned pepper and garlic. Shake well or blend until well combined. Pour dressing over shrimp; cover and refrigerate for 1 to 2 hours to blend flavors. To serve, cut avocados in halves, peel and remove pits; rub with lime or lemon juice and arrange each half on a bed of shredded lettuce on an individual salad plate. Fill with shrimp, drizzling any dressing remaining in bowl over lettuce. Garnish with cherry tomato halves. Makes 4 servings.

Citrus Squeezers

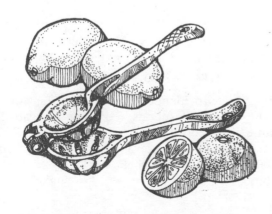

Fresh citrus juices, especially lime juice, are used abundantly in Mexican cooking. In Mexican markets you can find a somewhat crude looking but effective perforated hinged metal juicer designed to be just lime-sized.

An ordinary glass or plastic reamer works equally well for limes, oranges, lemons and grapefruit. An aluminum juicer that strains out seeds (if any) and pulp while positioned over another container is also a good choice.

If you are really using citrus fruits in quantity, you may find it worthwhile to invest in an electric juicer or a juice-squeezing attachment for your electric mixer.

Here is an elegant first course salad of sliced hearts of palm and tiny shrimp in a vinaigrette dressing, accented by hard-cooked eggs and tomatoes. Canned hearts of palm from Latin America can be found in shops and supermarkets that feature imported foods.

Hearts of Palm Salad   *(Palmito Vinagreta)*

2   tablespoons salad oil
1   tablespoon olive oil
4   teaspoons lime or lemon juice
1   clove garlic, minced or pressed
½   teaspoon *each* salt and oregano
¼   teaspoon sugar
    Dash cayenne
1   can (14 oz.) hearts of palm,
       drained and sliced in ¼-inch-
       thick rounds
¼   pound tiny peeled cooked shrimp
    Shredded iceberg lettuce
1   medium tomato, cut in wedges
1   hard-cooked egg, sliced

In a small blender container or tightly covered jar, combine salad and olive oils, lime or lemon juice, garlic, salt, oregano, sugar and cayenne. Blend or shake together until well blended. Mix lightly with hearts of palm and shrimp. Cover and refrigerate for 1 to 2 hours to blend flavors. Serve hearts of palm mixture atop shredded lettuce on chilled plates, garnished with tomato wedges and egg slices. Makes 4 servings.

Jaliscan Zucchini Salad   *(Ensalada de Calabazita)*

Raw zucchini has an intriguing, crisp texture and this simple salad makes the most of that. A sprinkling of fresh cilantro over the top is an effective final touch.

4   medium zucchini (1¼ to 1½ lbs.),
       scrubbed and thinly sliced
1   small mild red onion, thinly
       sliced and separated into rings
    Oil and Vinegar Dressing (recipe
       follows)
    Leaf lettuce
1   cup halved cherry tomatoes
    Chopped fresh cilantro or
       parsley, for garnish

Lightly mix zucchini, onion and Oil and Vinegar Dressing. Line a salad bowl with lettuce; fill with zucchini mixture. Scatter tomato halves over the top; sprinkle with chopped cilantro or parsley. Serve immediately. Makes 6 servings.

Oil and Vinegar Dressing: In blender container or jar combine 1/3 cup salad oil, 2 tablespoons red wine vinegar, 1 tablespoon fresh lime or lemon juice, 1/2 teaspoon salt, 1/4 teaspoon *each* sugar and crumbled oregano and 1/8 teaspoon seasoned pepper. Whirl in blender or shake in tightly covered jar until well combined. (If made ahead, whirl or shake again just before mixing with salad.)

Fresh coriander accents the oil and vinegar dressing of this avocado, lettuce and tomato salad.

Avocado and Tomato Salad   *(Ensalada de Aguacate)*

3 tablespoons salad oil
1 tablespoon cider vinegar
1 clove garlic, minced or pressed
½ teaspoon salt
¼ teaspoon dry mustard
2 tablespoons chopped fresh cilan-
    tro, *or* 1 teaspoon dried
    cilantro
    Dash cayenne
3 cups torn romaine or leaf
    lettuce
3 cups torn iceberg lettuce
3 green onions, thinly sliced
1 medium tomato, cut in 8 wedges
1 avocado, halved, peeled and
    sliced crosswise

In a small blender container or tightly covered jar, combine salad oil, vinegar, garlic, salt, dry mustard, cilantro and cayenne. Blend or shake together until smooth and well combined. Mix dressing lightly with greens, onions, tomato and avocado. Serve immediately on chilled salad plates. Makes 4 to 6 servings.

Mexican Seafood Salad   *(Ensalada de Mariscos)*

This seafood salad can be either a first course or a luncheon main dish with *bolillos* (see page 100) and a full-bodied Mexican beer. In Mexico the seafoods might also include tiny raw oysters, abalone or cold poached fish, but you can keep it as simple as shrimp and crab meat.

½ pound tiny peeled cooked shrimp
½ pound cooked crab meat, flaked
    and cartilage removed
¼ cup *each* thinly sliced celery and
    green onions (use part of tops)
2 tablespoons chopped fresh cilantro
    or parsley
    La Playa Dressing (recipe follows)
    Shredded iceberg lettuce
2 hard-cooked eggs, cut in wedges
    Lime wedges

Lightly mix shrimp, crab meat, celery, green onions, cilantro and 1/2 cup of the dressing. Mound seafood mixture on shredded lettuce on 4 to 6 chilled salad plates. Drizzle each with a little more dressing. Garnish with hard-cooked egg and lime wedges. Serve with additional dressing to add to taste. Makes 4 to 6 servings.

La Playa Dressing: In a bowl mix until smooth 1/2 cup *each* mayonnaise and sour cream, 1/3 cup chili sauce, 2 tablespoons *each* chopped stuffed green olives and fresh orange juice, 1 to 2 tablespoons *picante* sauce and 1/4 teaspoon garlic salt. Chill for 30 minutes or longer to blend flavors. Makes about 1-1/2 cups.

Cilantro . . . an Essential Seasoning You Can Grow

One of the most distinctive flavors in the dazzling spectrum of herbs and spices used in Mexican cooking is that of *cilantro* (say *see*-LAHN-*trow*). It seasons many of the world's cuisines—Chinese, Indian and Portuguese are just a few others. It is also known as fresh coriander, Chinese parsley and Mexican parsley. Outwardly cilantro looks like a broadleafed parsley, but it tastes much different.

You can find it in pungent bunches in Mexican and Chinese markets, and it is also available dried (look for it in the Spice Islands line). When you bring home a bunch of cilantro, rinse it lightly, then stand the stems in about 2 inches of water in a container. Cover the leaves with a plastic bag and the cilantro will stay perky in the refrigerator for several days.

Cilantro can also be grown in a pot or window box in a sunny place. Just plant whole coriander seeds from your spice shelf, or look for Chinese parsley seeds in an Oriental hardware or garden supply store. As the plants grow, pinch back the leaves frequently to prevent them from flowering and going to seed. In an herb garden, the plants will eventually reseed themselves.

EGGS FOR ANY TIME OF DAY

Some of the most colorful dishes created in the Mexican kitchen involve eggs. If you're farsighted enough to prepare the sauces ahead, these egg dishes are terrific for breakfast. They also make fine late brunches, festive lunches and family suppers.

The best known egg dish from Mexico must be *huevos rancheros* (say WAY-*vohs rahn*-CHAIR-*ohs*), usually translated as "ranch-style eggs." There are many versions, but this seems to be the most typical—fried eggs atop lightly fried tortillas, with a mildly piquant tomato sauce and a sprinkling of cheese. A garnish of avocado slices makes it all seem a little more special.

Ranch-Style Eggs   *(Huevos Rancheros)*

1   medium onion, chopped
1   tablespoon lard
1   clove garlic, minced or pressed
1   canned green chile, seeded and
       chopped
1   can (1 lb.) tomatoes
½   teaspoon *each* salt and dried
       cilantro
¼   teaspoon sugar
1   teaspoon chile powder
8   corn tortillas
    Oil for frying
8   eggs
    Shredded Monterey jack or white
       Cheddar cheese, or crumbled
       Feta cheese
1   avocado, sliced

In a medium frying pan cook onion in heated lard until soft but not browned. Mix in garlic, green chile, tomatoes and their liquid (break tomatoes up with a fork), salt, cilantro, sugar and chile powder. Bring to boiling, cover, reduce heat and simmer for 45 minutes. Uncover and cook for about 5 minutes longer, stirring occasionally, to reduce sauce slightly (this much can be done ahead and reheated).

To serve, fry tortillas in a large frying pan in about 1/2 inch of oil until limp; *or*, if you prefer, fry them until crisp and lightly browned. Drain on paper towels and keep warm in a 250° oven. Pour off most of the oil. Fry eggs until done to taste. For each serving, arrange two warm fried tortillas on a large plate. Top each with an egg, then spoon on hot tomato sauce. Sprinkle with cheese. Garnish with avocado slices. Accompany with Refried Beans (see page 92). Makes 4 servings, 2 tortillas each.

Scrambled Eggs, Mexican Style   *(Huevos a la Mexicana)*

Huevos a la Mexicana involve some of the same elements as the preceding recipe: eggs, onions, tomatoes and green chiles. But when the eggs are scrambled, how different is the end product!

1   small onion, finely chopped
3   tablespoons butter, margarine or
       salad oil
6   eggs
2   tablespoons water
½   teaspoon salt
2   small green Serrano chiles, seeded
       and finely chopped, *or* ¼ cup
       chopped canned green chiles
1   small tomato, seeded and chopped

Cook onion in heated butter, margarine or oil in a medium frying pan, stirring occasionally, until tender and lightly browned. Beat eggs with water and salt until well combined. Add chopped green chile and tomato to onions. Add egg mixture and cook over low heat, stirring gently, until eggs are just set but still moist. Serve immediately on warm plates, accompanied by toasted buttered *bolillos* (see page 100) or warm corn tortillas and refried beans. Makes 3 to 4 servings.

It seems that just about any Mexican dish can be rolled up in a warm tortilla and eaten as a sort of soft taco. Here's one in which scrambled eggs can be enjoyed this way. From Sonora, it uses flour tortillas.

Scrambled Eggs and Beef   *(Huevos Machaca)*

---

2   tablespoons butter or margarine
1   tablespoon salad oil
1   small onion, finely chopped
8   eggs
2   tablespoons water
¾   teaspoon salt
1   California (Anaheim) green chile, seeded and finely chopped *or* ¼ cup chopped canned green chiles
1   small tomato, seeded and chopped
    Shredded Beef (recipe follows)
    Warm flour tortillas

In a heavy frying pan, heat together butter and oil. In it cook onion until soft but not browned. Meanwhile, beat eggs with water and salt until well combined. To onion add chile, tomato and Shredded Beef. Cook, stirring, until beef is heated through. Add eggs. Cook over low heat, stirring gently and tipping and tilting pan to allow uncooked eggs to flow underneath, until the eggs are just set but still moist. Serve on warm plates, accompanied by warm flour tortillas in which to roll up egg mixture. Serve with Refried Beans (see page 92). Makes 4 servings.

Shredded Beef: In 1 tablespoon heated lard in a small frying pan, brown 1/4 pound beef stew meat, cut in small cubes. Sprinkle with 1/2 teaspoon *each* salt and chile powder and a dash of garlic powder. Add 1 small tomato, peeled and chopped, and 1/4 cup water. Bring to boiling, reduce heat, cover tightly and simmer for 1-1/2 to 2 hours, until beef is very tender; uncover and continue cooking until liquid is gone. Use two forks to divide meat into shreds.

A fresh tomato sauce underneath and a generous blanket of melted cheese on top make another special treatment for fried eggs. Served in individual casseroles straight from the broiler, this dish is good with refried beans and crusty rolls on the side.

Fried Eggs with Cheese and Tomato Sauce   *(Huevos con Queso)*

1   medium onion, slivered
1   tablespoon lard
4   large ripe tomatoes, peeled and
        chopped
1   clove garlic, minced or pressed
1   canned green chile, chopped
¼   cup chopped fresh cilantro, *or*
        1 tablespoon dried cilantro
2   teaspoons salt
½   teaspoon ground cumin
¼   teaspoon sugar
8   eggs
2   tablespoons butter or margarine
1   cup shredded Monterey jack
        cheese

Cook onion in heated lard in a medium-sized frying pan until soft but not browned. Add tomatoes and their liquid, garlic, green chile, cilantro, salt, cumin and sugar. Bring to boiling, cover tightly, reduce heat and simmer for 30 minutes. Uncover and continue cooking, stirring occasionally, for about 10 minutes longer until sauce is thick. Divide sauce into four shallow individual casseroles; keep warm. Fry eggs in butter until done to taste. Arrange 2 fried eggs in each casserole. Sprinkle with cheese. Place under broiler and broil about 6 inches from heat until cheese is melted, bubbling and lightly browned. Makes 4 servings.

Here is an egg dish reflecting the Mayan style of cooking that can be enjoyed in Yucatán. It has several elements—fried tortillas, sautéed ham, black beans, a tomato sauce, fried eggs and a light topping of shredded cheese. If you plan ahead and have all the components assembled and ready to use, it is not as complicated as it sounds. This dish is named for a town between Mérida and the tip of the peninsula.

Fried Eggs, Motul Style   *(Huevos Motuleños)*

8 corn tortillas
   Salad oil for deep frying
1 cup diced cooked ham
3 tablespoons butter, margarine or
      salad oil
   Refried Black Beans (see page 92)
   Spicy Tomato Sauce (recipe
      follows)
½ cup frozen peas, thawed
8 eggs
½ cup shredded white Cheddar or
      Fontinella cheese

Fry tortillas, one or two at a time, in oil heated to 350° to 375° in a heavy frying pan, electric skillet or Chinese wok, turning once or twice, until tortillas are crisp and lightly browned. Drain, place on paper towels, and keep warm in a 200° oven while completing the dish.

Brown ham lightly in 1 tablespoon of the butter in a large frying pan; remove from pan and keep warm. Reheat beans in another pan. To hot Tomato Sauce, add peas and cook, uncovered, for 3 to 5 minutes. Cook eggs to desired doneness in remaining butter in pan in which ham was cooked. To serve, spread crisp hot tortillas with beans. Top each tortilla with a fried egg. Arrange, two to a serving, on warm plates. Sprinkle with ham. Spoon on Tomato Sauce. Sprinkle with cheese. Serve accompanied by Fried Bananas (see page 98), if you wish. Makes 4 servings.

Spicy Tomato Sauce: Coarsely chop tomatoes from 1 can (14-1/2 oz.) Italian-style pear-shaped tomatoes. Cook 1 medium onion, finely chopped, in 1 tablespoon salad oil or olive oil in a heavy 1-1/2-quart saucepan. Add chopped tomatoes and their liquid; 1 clove garlic, minced or pressed; 1/2 teaspoon crumbled oregano; 1/4 teaspoon ground cumin; 1 teaspoon salt, and 2 canned green chiles, chopped. Bring to boiling, cover, reduce heat and simmer for 30 minutes. Uncover and boil gently, stirring occasionally, until sauce is reduced to about 1-1/2 cups.

A good example of the way in which Spanish and native Mexican influences have been mixed in today's Mexican cooking can be seen in the style of omelet served in Mexico. It is filled with crisply fried shredded potatoes and served with a tangy tomato sauce. Both potatoes and tomatoes were unknown in Europe until they were brought there from the Americas.

Spanish Potato-Filled Omelet   *(Omelet Española)*

2   medium-sized new potatoes
1   teaspoon salt
     Seasoned pepper
¼   cup butter or margarine
1   tablespoon salad oil
6   eggs
2   tablespoons water
     Quick Tomato Sauce (recipe
        follows)

Peel and shred potatoes (you should have about 2 cups); mix lightly with 1/2 teaspoon of the salt and a dash of seasoned pepper. In a medium-sized frying pan heat 2 tablespoons of the butter with the salad oil. Spread potato mixture in pan and cook slowly over moderately low heat, until potatoes are well browned; turn and continue cooking until second side is nicely browned and potatoes are done. Keep potatoes warm while preparing omelets.

Beat together eggs, water, remaining 1/2 teaspoon salt and a dash of seasoned pepper. For each omelet, in an individual 8-inch omelet pan, heat 1 tablespoon of the remaining butter. Pour in half of the egg mixture and cook over moderately high heat, lifting egg mixture to allow uncooked portion to flow underneath, until set but still moist. Drizzle with a little of the Tomato Sauce; spoon on half of the potatoes. Roll or fold omelet and slip out onto a warm plate. Spoon remaining sauce over omelets. Accompany with browned hot Italian-style sausages or other pork sausages. Makes 2 omelets.

Quick Tomato Sauce: Cook 1/4 cup chopped onion in 1 tablespoon salad oil until soft but not browned. Mix in 1 can (8 oz.) tomato sauce; 1 canned green chile, chopped; 1/4 teaspoon garlic powder, and 3/4 teaspoon chile powder. Cover and simmer for 10 minutes.

The Right Pan for the Job

Omelets are easier to make when you have the proper pan for the job. A classic omelet pan is shallow with rounded sides sloping gradually into the bottom. This special shape enables you to slide the finished omelet out as effortlessly as a skilled chef.

This specifically designed pan is available in several sizes and made from a variety of materials. An 8-inch pan is a good size for individual omelets; larger sizes up to 10 inches can be used to make an omelet for two or three. An omelet made in a much larger pan than that becomes somewhat unwieldy.

Spun steel is the material used for the omelet pans in most restaurants. It should be well seasoned to prevent rust and to give the pan a surface that resists sticking. Follow the manufacturer's directions or this method: Wash the pan in mild detergent and dry thoroughly. Apply a light coating of vegetable oil over the cooking surface with a paper towel and heat at medium temperature until the pan takes on a brown color. Let the pan cool a few minutes before applying another light coat of oil and heating again until the pan darkens a little more. After seasoning, do not scour the pan or it will require re-seasoning.

A medium-weight aluminum also makes a fine omelet pan in the traditional shape. Aluminum pans can be washed after each use, as they will not rust. Nonstick coatings are not necessary, but if your omelet pan has one, be careful to use a wooden or plastic spatula with it so that you don't scratch the coating.

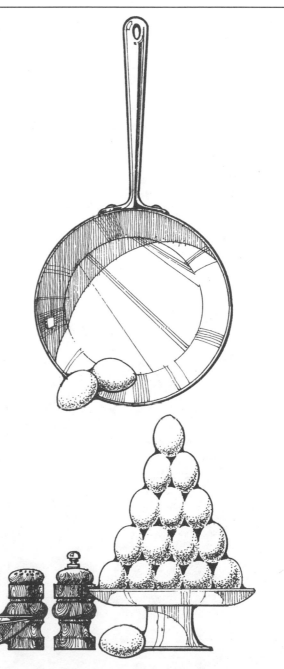

A meatless yet very substantial main dish is this plump omelet filled with green chiles, cumin flavored onions and an abundance of melty Monterey jack cheese.

Cheese and Green Chile Omelet

¼ cup butter or margarine
1 medium onion, finely chopped
¼ teaspoon ground cumin
1 can (4 oz.) diced green chiles
6 eggs
2 tablespoons water
½ teaspoon salt
   Dash seasoned pepper
1 cup shredded Monterey jack
   cheese
   Radish roses, for garnish

For filling, in 2 tablespoons of the butter, cooked chopped onion until tender and lightly browned. Stir in cumin and green chiles; keep warm.

Beat together eggs, water, salt and seasoned pepper. Heat remaining 2 tablespoons butter in a 9-1/2 to 10-inch omelet pan. Pour in egg mixture and cook over moderately high heat, lifting eggs to allow uncooked portion to flow underneath, until set but still moist. Cover with green chile and onion mixture, then sprinkle with about 2/3 cup of the cheese. Roll or fold omelet and slip out onto a warm plate. Sprinkle remaining cheese over omelet; place under broiler for a few seconds to melt cheese. Garnish with radish roses. Serve immediately. Makes 2 to 3 servings.

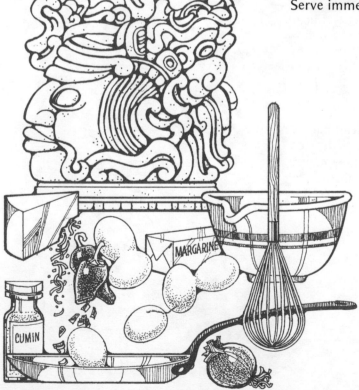

MEATS FROM MEXICAN KITCHENS

Meat plays more of a supporting than a starring role in Mexican cooking. But when it is featured, such as in one of the famed grilled or barbecued dishes, or in a rich stew or soup that has been simmered for hours, the results can be spectacular.

Some Mexican soups are so hearty, so satisfying and so complete that the soup alone can be a full meal. This meatball soup is a good example. All it needs is the accent of chopped fresh green chiles or a squeeze of lime, a buttered tortilla and perhaps a frosty glass of beer. The meatballs can be seasoned with one of two herbs, preferably fresh—spearmint (which was the *yerba buena* that gave San Francisco its previous name) or cilantro.

Meal-in-One Meatball Soup   *(Sopa de Albóndigas)*

1   large can (47 oz.) or about 6 cups
    homemade regular-strength
    chicken broth
1   medium onion, cut in 6 wedges,
    then thinly slivered
1   clove garlic, minced or pressed
1   stalk celery, finely chopped
    (including leaves)
1   can (8 oz.) tomato sauce
    Meatballs (recipe follows)
1   medium-sized new potato, diced
2   carrots, thinly sliced
1   large tomato, cut in about ½-inch
    cubes
2   cups shredded cabbage
1   medium zucchini, thinly sliced
    Salt
    Finely chopped, seeded fresh
    jalapeño or California (Ana-
    heim) or canned green chiles
    Lime or lemon wedges

In a 5-1/2 to 6-quart kettle or Dutch oven, heat together chicken broth, onion, garlic, celery and tomato sauce; when mixture boils, reduce heat, cover and simmer for 30 minutes. Add meatballs, potato and carrots. Bring to a gentle boil, then cover again and simmer for 45 minutes longer, until potatoes are tender and rice in meatballs is cooked. Add tomato, cabbage and zucchini. Simmer, uncovered, for about 10 minutes longer, just until soup boils again and zucchini is tender-crisp. Salt to taste. Serve with chopped chiles and lime or lemon wedges to add at the table to taste. Accompany with hot buttered corn or flour tortillas. Makes 6 servings.

Meatballs: Lightly beat 1 egg in a medium-sized mixing bowl. Mix in 1 clove garlic, minced or pressed; 1 teaspoon salt; 1/8 teaspoon cayenne pepper; 2 tablespoons chopped fresh mint or 2 teaspoons dried mint, *or* 2 tablespoons chopped fresh cilantro or 2 teaspoons dried cilantro; 2 tablespoons uncooked long-grain rice; and 1 pound lean ground beef. Mix lightly. Shape into 1-inch balls.

The flavor of this tender beef stew is on the *picante* side. If you prefer milder flavor, omit the dried red pepper.

Mexican Beef Stew *(Filete Mexicana)*

2 pounds lean boneless beef stew
    meat, cut in 1-inch cubes
  Salt and flour
2 tablespoons lard
2 medium onions, chopped
1 clove garlic, minced or pressed
1 carrot, thinly sliced
1 small can (4 oz.) green chiles,
    seeded and cut in strips
1 small dried red pepper, crushed
    (optional)
¼ cup chopped fresh cilantro, *or*
    1½ teaspoons dried cilantro
1 cup regular-strength beef broth,
    canned or homemade
2 medium-sized new potatoes, cut
    in 1-inch chunks

Sprinkle beef cubes with salt; coat lightly with flour. In heated lard in a large deep frying pan, brown meat well (about one-third at a time) on all sides. When all the meat is browned, return it to the pan. Add onions, garlic, carrot and green chiles. Sprinkle with red pepper (if used) and cilantro. Pour on broth. Bring to boiling, cover, reduce heat and simmer for 2 hours; add potatoes and continue cooking for about 45 minutes longer, until meat and potatoes are very tender. Taste and add salt, if needed. Accompany with Refried Beans (see page 92) and warm corn tortillas. Makes 6 to 8 servings.

A Special Tool for Garlic

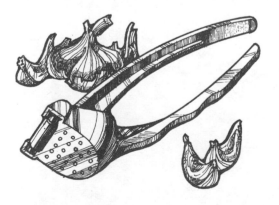

The perfume of garlic pervades many a Mexican specialty. If you enjoy this seasoning and use it frequently, you will probably find a garlic press a useful tool. It reduces each clove of garlic to a pungent purée, saving you the considerable work of a lot of fine chopping.

It has been said that, when necessary, a tortilla can be the plate, the fork and even the napkin for many Mexican dishes. Here is one that really is most enjoyable when you eat it in that fashion. The quickly sautéed steak strips and onions, briskly seasoned with green chiles, are served covered with a blanket of freshly made corn tortillas that serve two purposes—to keep the food warm, and to provide a wrapper for the meat and onions. Customarily, this dish is eaten with the fingers.

Farmer-Style Steak Strips and Onions   *(Filete a la Campesina)*

2   tablespoons *each* butter or margarine and salad oil
3   medium onions, thinly sliced and separated into rings
1   clove garlic, minced or pressed
½   teaspoon crumbled oregano
8   small green Serrano chiles, *or* ¼ cup chopped canned green chiles
1½   pounds boneless top sirloin steak, about ¾ inch thick
Salt and pepper
Warm tortillas

In a large frying pan, heat 1 tablespoon *each* of the butter and oil. Mix in onions, garlic and oregano. Cook over low to moderate heat, stirring occasionally, until onions are tender and transparent and beginning to brown, about 20 minutes; remove from pan and keep onions warm. While onions are cooking, toast Serrano chiles (if used) on an ungreased griddle until blistered on all sides; remove from heat, and reserve.

Cut steak across the grain into bite-sized strips about 2 inches long and 1/4 inch thick; sprinkle with salt and pepper. Add remaining 1 tablespoon *each* butter and oil to pan in which onions were cooked; increase heat to high. Cook steak strips quickly, about one-third at a time, browning on both sides and adding them to onions as they brown. When all steak is cooked, return steak and onion mixture to frying pan with chiles. Cook, stirring, just until mixture is heated through. Serve in a warm deep platter with tortillas arranged to completely cover the top. Accompany with Refried Black Beans (see page 92). Makes 4 servings.

It would be a mistake to give the impression that tortillas are the only bread of Mexico. Mexican bakers excel at oven-baked breads as well, and the crusty rolls and loaves resembling French bread are marvelous. One of the best ways to enjoy them is made into a sandwich with tender, quickly cooked steak strips, onions and guacamole. Such a sandwich is popular in Guadalajara.

'Pepito' Steak and Onion Sandwich   *(Pepito Lonche de Filete)*

2 medium onions, thinly sliced and separated into rings
2 tablespoons *each* butter or margarine and peanut oil or salad oil
1 pound boneless top sirloin, 1 inch thick
4 warm *bolillos* (see page 100) or crusty French rolls
   Salt
½ cup guacamole (see page 15) or frozen avocado dip, thawed
1 medium tomato, sliced
   Green chile salsa (optional)

In a large frying pan cook onions in 1 tablespoon *each* of the butter and oil, stirring occasionally over moderate heat until onions are limp, tender and beginning to brown, about 20 minutes; remove to an ovenproof dish and keep onions warm. Cut steak across the grain into 1/4-inch-thick strips. In same pan in which onions were cooked, heat remaining butter and oil over high heat until foamy. Cook steak strips, about half at a time, just until browned on both sides. Split warm rolls. Cover bottom halves of rolls with steak strips; sprinkle with salt. Top with guacamole, cooked onions and tomato slices. Drizzle with green chile salsa to taste. Cover with top halves of warm rolls. Serve sandwiches immediately with very cold beer. Makes 4 sandwiches.

Carne asada (say CAR-*neh ah*-SAH-*dah*) appears frequently on Mexican menus. The term has an unspecific meaning—roast meat. As served in restaurants it is usually barbecued or grilled and the meat takes the form of a thin, well seasoned boneless steak, cooked quickly to retain its juicy tenderness. Skirt steaks adapt well to this style of cooking.

Spicy Barbecued Skirt Steak *(Carne Asada a la Tampiqueña)*

2 tablespoons salad oil
1 tablespoon lime or lemon juice
2 small dried red peppers, coarsely chopped
1 clove garlic, minced or pressed
½ teaspoon salt
1 pound beef skirt steak
½ cup *each* slivered red and green bell peppers or California (Anaheim) green chiles and mild onion

In a small blender jar combine oil, lime or lemon juice, dried red peppers, garlic and salt; whirl until smooth and well combined. If skirt steaks are rolled into pinwheels, unroll them. Meat should be in the form of strips about 3 inches wide and 6 to 8 inches long. Place meat flat in a shallow baking dish, and brush both sides well with marinade; cover and refrigerate for 2 to 4 hours. Broil or barbecue over low coals until steak is nicely browned but still rare in center, about 3 minutes per side. Serve with a mixture of red and green pepper and onion strips. Accompany with Refried Beans, rice and quesadillas (page 35) or cheese tacos (page 16). Makes 2 to 3 servings.

Barbecued Flank Steak with Spicy Tomato Sauce *(Carne Asada California)*

This style of carne asada, milder in flavor and using flank steak, is more typical of that served in California's Mexican restaurants.

1 tablespoon salad oil
2 cloves garlic, minced or pressed
1 teaspoon chile powder
1½ pounds flank steak
Salt
Tomato and Green Chile Sauce (recipe follows)

Mix oil, garlic and chile powder. Drizzle the mixture evenly over both sides of flank steak, cover and refrigerate for 1 to 3 hours. Barbecue steak over low coals, or broil it, until nicely browned but still rare in center, about 8 minutes on each side. Salt to taste. Slice across the grain in thin diagonal slices. Top with sauce. Serve immediately. Accompany with Refried Beans and Red Rice (see page 96). Makes 4 servings.

Tomato and Green Chile Sauce: Cut 1 medium onion into sixths, then slice each wedge thinly. In a 1-1/2 to 2-quart saucepan, heat 1 tablespoon olive oil or salad oil; in it cook onion until soft but not browned. Mix in 1 clove garlic, minced or pressed; 1/2 teaspoon chile powder; 1 small can (4 oz.) green chiles, seeded and chopped, and 1 can (8 oz.) tomato sauce. Bring to boiling, cover, reduce heat and simmer for 20 minutes.

Chile is a word to start arguments. To many people it means a hearty dish of beef and red beans. In the vocabulary of Mexican cooking, it signifies a red or green pepper used for flavor—which can sometimes be very hot. This chile recipe does not have much to do with either of those definitions. It is a beef and pork stew in a savory green sauce, and there are no beans in it.

My favorite way with this stew was introduced to me years ago by a Texan. He brought a gigantic pot of a similar green chile, his own creation, to a beach picnic on the windswept northern California coast. We scooped up the chile, along with rice and toasted pine nuts, using warm flour tortillas. To this day, that is the way this chile tastes best to me.

Green Chile Con Carne   *(Chile Verde)*

1   pound boneless beef stew meat,
      cut in 1-inch cubes
2   pounds lean boneless pork butt,
      cut in 1-inch cubes
2   tablespoons lard
2   large onions, chopped
2   cloves garlic, minced or pressed
1   can (13 or 14 oz.) *tomatillos*
      (Mexican green tomatoes),
      cut in quarters
1   large can (7 oz.) green chiles,
      seeded and chopped
1   teaspoon ground cumin
¾   teaspoon crumbled oregano
¼   cup chopped fresh cilantro, *or*
      1 tablespoon dried cilantro
¾   cup water
     Salt
¼   cup toasted pine nuts or slivered
      almonds (directions follow)
     Chopped fresh cilantro or pars-
      ley, for garnish
     Warm flour tortillas
     Steamed rice
     Sliced avocado

Brown meats, about one-third at a time, in heated lard in a 5 to 6-quart Dutch oven. When all the meat is browned, pour off excess fat if necessary. Return meat to pan with any accumulated juices; add onions, garlic, tomatillos and their liquid, green chiles, cumin, oregano, cilantro and water. Bring to boiling, cover, reduce heat and simmer for 2-1/2 to 3 hours, until meat is very tender. Uncover and continue cooking at a gentle boil, stirring occasionally, until thickened to taste. Salt to taste. To serve, sprinkle with pine nuts and chopped cilantro. If you wish, use the chile as a filling for warm tortillas, with each person making his own using rice, the meat and avocado slices (in that order). Or, serve over rice in soup bowls with the suggested toppings. Makes 8 servings.

To toast pine nuts or almonds: Spread nuts in a shallow pan. Bake in a 350° oven for about 10 minutes, stirring once or twice, until lightly browned.

Here is another of those flavor-packed meal-in-one Mexican soups, this one made with black beans that cook to a unique purplish-brown color. Such beans are grown in the U.S. as well as in Mexico, and you should be able to find them in stores that have a good selection of dried beans in bulk. As an accompaniment, you might select the fresh zucchini salad on page 52.

Smoky Oaxacan Black Bean Soup *(Sopa de Frijoles Negros)*

1	pound (2 cups) black beans, rinsed and drained
9	cups water
2	tablespoons lard, salad oil, butter or margarine
2	stalks celery, finely chopped
2	medium onions, chopped
3	cloves garlic
2	smoked ham hocks (about 2 lbs.)
1	small dried red pepper, crushed
1	teaspoon ground coriander
¼	teaspoon ground cloves
	Salt, if needed
	Fried Tortilla Strips (directions follow)
	Crumbled Feta or shredded Monterey jack cheese

Place beans in a large bowl, add 4 cups of the water and let stand overnight (or, if you prefer, bring beans and the 4 cups water to boiling in a 4-quart kettle, boil briskly for 2 minutes, then remove from heat and let stand, covered, for 1 hour). Meanwhile, heat lard or other fat in a 5-1/2 to 6-quart kettle or Dutch oven. In it sauté celery and onions until soft; stir in garlic. Add ham hocks and remaining 5 cups water. Bring to boiling, cover, reduce heat and simmer until ham is very tender, about 3 hours. Remove ham hocks from broth, discard skin and bones, chop meat and return it to the soup (if you wish, you can do this much ahead, cover and refrigerate; skim off fat). To the soup add soaked beans and their liquid, crushed red pepper, coriander and cloves. Bring to boiling, cover, reduce heat and simmer for 3 to 3-1/2 hours, until beans are very tender. Taste and add salt, if needed. Serve topped with Fried Tortilla Strips and crumbled cheese. Makes 4 to 5 servings as a main course.

Fried Tortilla Strips: Cut 4 corn tortillas into strips 1/2 inch wide and 2 inches long. Pour salad oil or peanut oil to a depth of at least 1/2 inch in a heavy frying pan, electric skillet or Chinese wok; heat to a temperature of 350° to 375°. Fry tortilla strips, a few at a time, until crisp and lightly browned. Remove to paper towels to drain.

One of the most admired dishes of Yucatán is suckling pig or chicken cooked in an earthen pit lined with banana leaves. Known as *cochinita pibil* (or *pollo en pibil*), it takes its name from the pit or *pib*.

For most of us, either digging up the backyard or obtaining the requisite banana leaves presents a serious obstacle to preparing such a dish authentically. If you would like to taste an approximation of its flavors, however, here is a very much compromised version using boneless pork butt simmered on your range top. Swiss chard stands in for the banana leaves.

One of the seasonings used in this Mayan dish is *achiote*, also known as annatto. These are hard little crimson seeds which are elsewhere used to color margarine. They can be found in some Mexican-American grocery stores. The flavor of the meat will not be seriously impaired if you omit *achiote*, and a little turmeric will give a similar color.

Mayan Pork Packets

3½ pounds boneless pork butt roast
2 large onions, cut in wedges, then thinly sliced
3 cloves garlic, minced or pressed
1 can (1 lb.) tomatoes, coarsely chopped
Juice of 1 orange
2 teaspoons salt
½ teaspoon *each* crushed oregano and ground cumin
1 small dried red pepper, crushed
1 teaspoon *achiote* (annatto), optional
2 tablespoons cider vinegar
2 bunches Swiss chard (12 to 16 large leaves)

Place roast in a large deep kettle or Dutch oven. Around it add onions and garlic. Pour on tomatoes and their liquid and orange juice. Sprinkle with salt, oregano, cumin, crushed red pepper and *achiote* (if used). Bring to boiling, cover, reduce heat and simmer for 2-1/2 to 3 hours, until meat is very tender. Remove meat and let cool slightly. Skim fat from cooking liquid; bring to a gentle boil and cook, uncovered, until reduced and thickened, stirring occasionally, about 15 minutes. Meanwhile, separate pork into large chunks, discarding fat. Return meat to the thickened sauce; stir in vinegar. Taste and add salt, if needed. Remove from heat.

Cut off coarse ends of chard leaves. Steam them *just until* leaves begin to become limp, 1 to 2 minutes. Divide meat sauce into as many portions as you have chard leaves. Place each portion atop a chard leaf, fold in sides, and roll into a packet, beginning at broad end (this much can be done ahead and refrigerated).

To serve, arrange pork packets on a rack well above about 1 inch of boiling water to make a steamer; cover with a sheet of waxed paper. Cover pan and steam for about 20 minutes, until packets are heated through. Serve with rice. Makes 6 to 8 servings.

Mexican Chile Peppers

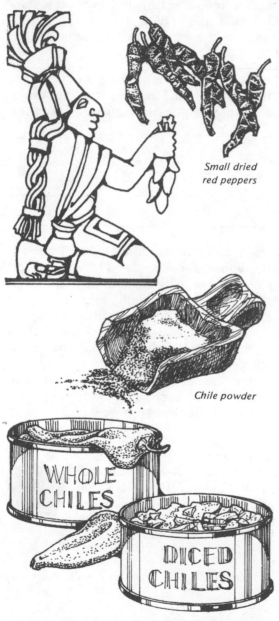

*Small dried
red peppers*

Chile powder

Canned green chiles

WHOLE
CHILES

DICED
CHILES

In a cuisine notable for its virtuosity in using spices and herbs, chiles are the most varied and distinctive Mexican seasoning. To visit a marketplace in Mexico is to realize how important they are. Dried chiles range widely in size, and in color from fiery crimson to purplish-black. An equally vast spectrum of fresh red and green chiles can be seen.

Authentically prepared Mexican dishes employ all these chiles, singly and in combination, with great precision. Their flavors vary considerably. A single taste of one variety may produce a sensation akin to a sideshow fire-eater's torch; others are truly mild and sweet.

Outside of Mexico, one seldom finds this much variety, even in centers of considerable Mexican-American population. Recipes in this book were tested using chiles fresh, dried and canned that seem to be most generally available. The following is a guide to the chiles specified:

California (Anaheim) chiles: They are mildly hot and average about 6 inches long; the color is a dark green or red. (A dark red dried form can sometimes be found in Mexican-American grocery stores.) This is the fresh chile used for *chiles rellenos.*

Canned green chiles: The canned version of the above. Mildly hot, available whole or chopped. With the seeds they are a little hotter than without.

Jalapeño chiles: Dark green, cylindrical, 2 to 3 inches long; quite hot tasting. Often pickled, canned or used in commercial hot sauces.

Small dried red peppers: These slender little chiles, 1 to 3 or 4 inches long, are fairly hot. Varieties from either Mexico or Japan can be used interchangeably. After working with chiles as hot as these, wash your hands thoroughly. The residue on your fingers, though unseen, can irritate your eyes or nose if you touch them.

Chile powder: As produced by most spice and herb companies, this mixture includes powdered dried chiles as well as other seasonings. You may have to sample several brands to find one you prefer. Chile powder is not the same as the packaged powdered chiles found in Mexican-American groceries, which can be quite hot depending on the variety of chile used.

Green (or red) bell peppers: Seen on just about every produce counter, these are the plump green peppers you use for salads and to stuff. They are not the least bit hot in flavor.

Serrano chiles: These tiny cylindrical, dark green chiles are 1 to 2 inches long and have a *very, very* hot flavor. They pack a real wallop for their size. Use them sparingly and chop them very finely to spread the heat around. After working with these chiles, wash your hands thoroughly. The residue can be very irritating to your eyes and nose.

Yellow wax peppers: Fat, triangular peppers, 2 to 3 inches long, with a flavor mid-way in the heat spectrum—hotter than a California green chile, but less so than a Serrano.

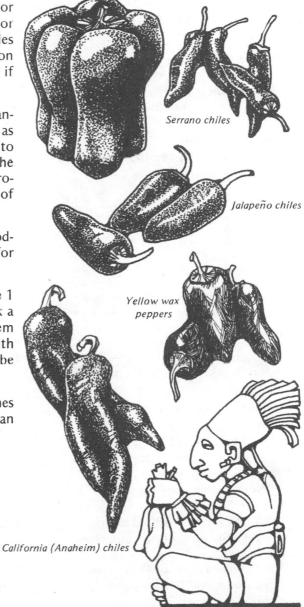

Green (or red) bell peppers

Serrano chiles

Jalapeño chiles

Yellow wax peppers

California (Anaheim) chiles

Cooking thinly sliced pork steaks in the flavorsome drippings of chorizo sausages imparts a splendid taste. Guacamole makes a fine sauce, if you wish.

Piquant Pork Steaks *(Carne Adobada)*

2 chorizo or linguiça sausages
    (about 6 oz.)
2 pounds boneless pork butt,
    sliced in ½-inch-thick steaks
  Salt
2 tablespoons white vinegar
  Guacamole (see page 15)

Remove sausage casings and crumble the meat into a large frying pan. Cook slowly, stirring, over moderately low heat until the sausage is nicely browned and crisp. With a slotted spoon, remove the cooked sausage; reserve the drippings in the pan. Refrigerate or freeze the cooked sausage for another use, such as in scrambled eggs or refried beans or for a taco filling. Slowly cook the pork steaks in the chorizo drippings, until nicely browned on both sides, a total of 20 to 30 minutes. Remove pork steaks to a warm serving platter; sprinkle with salt. Pour off and discard fat in pan. Add vinegar to pan and cook, stirring to loosen brown particles; pour over pork steaks. Serve with guacamole, warm tortillas and refried beans or rice. Makes 6 servings.

Mayan Lamb-Stuffed Cheese Casserole *(Queso Relleno con Carnero)*

Unlike most familiar dishes filled *with* cheese, this one—if made authentically—involves hollowing out a small cheese and filling it with a spicy ground lamb stuffing. To simplify this Mayan specialty, you can make layers of shredded cheese in a casserole with the meat mixture in the middle.

1 pound ground lamb, crumbled
1 large onion, finely chopped
1 clove garlic, minced or pressed
1 large tomato, peeled and chopped
½ cup chopped pimiento-stuffed
    green olives
¼ cup seedless raisins
½ teaspoon *each* crumbled dried
    oregano and ground cinnamon
  Dash cayenne
2 hard-cooked eggs, finely chopped
3 cups shredded Monterey jack
    cheese

In a large frying pan cook lamb over moderately high heat until it begins to release its drippings. Stir in onion and garlic; cook, stirring occasionally, until lamb is browned and onion is tender. Spoon off excess fat, if necessary. Stir in chopped tomato, olives, raisins, oregano, cinnamon and cayenne. Cover, reduce heat and simmer for 30 minutes. Uncover and continue cooking for about 10 minutes longer, until most of the liquid is gone. Mix in hard-cooked eggs. Sprinkle a shallow 6- to 8-cup casserole evenly with half of the shredded cheese. Spread meat mixture over cheese. Cover with remaining cheese. Bake in a 450° oven until cheese is bubbly and lightly browned, 10 to 15 minutes. Makes 4 to 6 servings.

Barbacoa can be found in various styles all over Mexico. Done in the traditional manner, the meat is cooked in a pit dug in the ground and lined with hot stones and leaves, somewhat like a Hawaiian luau. On special occasions the meat is *cabrito*—a young goat. If you have ever had the good fortune to taste skillfully cooked goat, you know that the flavor is similar to the most tender lamb.

To get an idea of the pleasures of a Mexican *barbacoa*, try this barbecued lamb shoulder roast. The meat is first simmered and then finished on a covered barbecue to crisp the skin and give the meat a smoky flavor. It's most appealing served with plenty of warm tortillas and a selection of condiments.

Barbecued Lamb, Mexican Style *(Barbacoa Rica de Carnero)*

Lamb shoulder roast (4½ to 5 lbs.)
1   can (1 lb.) tomatoes
2   cups water
2   teaspoons salt
½   teaspoon *each* crumbled oregano, ground cumin and ground coriander
1   small dried red pepper, crushed
2   medium onions, finely chopped
1   clove garlic, minced or pressed
1   carrot, shredded
1   can (8 oz.) tomato sauce
    Warm corn tortillas
    Lime wedges, thinly sliced green onions, chopped fresh jalapeño chiles or canned green chiles, and green taco sauce
    Refried Black Beans (see page 92)

Place roast in a deep 4-1/2 to 5-quart kettle or Dutch oven. Add tomatoes (broken up with a fork), water, salt, herbs, red pepper, onions, garlic and carrot. Bring to boiling, cover, reduce heat and simmer for 2-1/2 to 3 hours, until meat is tender. Remove roast, reserving cooking liquid. Skim fat from cooking liquid; add tomato sauce and bring to boiling. Cook, uncovered, stirring occasionally, until liquid is thickened and reduced to about 1 quart (this much can be done ahead, and the roast and sauce refrigerated separately).

About 1 hour before serving, place roast in a foil pan on grill over glowing coals in a covered barbecue. Cover and cook, basting occasionally with sauce, until roast is well browned and heated through, about 1 hour. Reheat sauce. Carve roast into generous chunks, place in a casserole, and pour sauce over. Serve chunks of the meat and sauce onto individual plates. Eat by cutting or tearing off pieces of meat, placing in warm tortillas and seasoning to taste with lime juice, green onions, chopped chiles and/or taco sauce. Accompany with Refried Black Beans. Makes 6 servings.

A Barbecue Grill That's Almost an Oven

With a covered barbecue, you can cook many foods that are not adaptable to a simple charcoal grill. A barbecue cart or kettle with a cover can be large enough to accommodate sizeable roasts, chickens and turkeys. Use an oven thermometer to keep track of the temperature, adding fuel if it drops too low.

Large cuts of meat cooking in a covered barbecue require a drip pan, either on the grill or just below the meat (with the charcoal arranged in a ring around it).

Fruit and sweet spices are often found in tantalizing combinations with meat in Mexican main dishes. These lamb chops, served with a sweet-sour raisin sauce, are a good example.

Broiled Lamb Chops with Spiced Raisin Sauce *(Chuletas de Cordero a la Parrilla con Salsa de Pasas)*

1   teaspoon *each* coarse or Kosher
    salt and grated orange rind
    Juice of 1 small lime
¼   teaspoon *each* ground cloves and
    crushed anise seeds
    Dash cayenne
1   clove garlic, minced or pressed
4   to 6 thick lamb rib chops
    (1¼ to 1½ lbs.)
¼   cup raisins
    Juice of 1 orange
2   tablespoons brown sugar
½   teaspoon cornstarch
¼   cup tequila
1   teaspoon red wine vinegar

In a small bowl, mix together salt, orange rind, lime juice, cloves, anise, cayenne and garlic. Place lamb chops in a shallow casserole and drizzle about half of the seasoning mixture over chops. Cover and refrigerate for about 1 hour. Meanwhile, place raisins and orange juice in a saucepan and add remaining seasoning mixture. Let stand until ready to make sauce.

Arrange lamb chops on rack in a broiler pan. Broil about 4 inches from heat, turning once, until nicely browned on both sides, 12 to 15 minutes in all. Meanwhile, stir brown sugar, cornstarch and tequila into raisin mixture. Bring to boiling, stirring, and cook until thickened and clear. Mix in vinegar. Place lamb chops on a serving platter and spoon raisin sauce over chops. Serve with fluffy rice. Makes 2 to 3 servings, 2 lamb chops each.

POULTRY IN A MEXICAN MANNER

Chicken and turkey play a prominent part in the Mexican diet. Many of the pre-Columbian patterns of seasonings persist to this day in such classic Mexican sauces for poultry as *mole* and *pipian*—made with sesame or anise seeds, chocolate, sweet spices and pumpkin or sunflower seed kernels. It can be a delightful adventure in new flavors to try some of these unusual Mexican creations.

Here is an appealing chicken dish from Puerto Vallarta. It makes a nice family meal with rice and crisp raw vegetables such as sticks or slices of cucumber, celery and perhaps that curious Mexican root vegetable, *jicama* (say HEE-*cah-ma*).

Spicy Chicken with Tomatoes and Green Chiles   *(Pollo a la Plaza)*

---

1   frying chicken (2½ to 3 lbs.),
      quartered
    Salt, pepper, cinnamon and flour
2   tablespoons salad oil or peanut oil
2   medium onions, thinly sliced
      and separated into rings
1   clove garlic, minced or pressed
1   can (1 lb.) tomatoes, broken up
      with a fork
1   small can (4 oz.) green chiles,
      seeded and chopped
½   teaspoon cumin seed, crushed
¼   teaspoon ground cloves
    Thinly sliced green onion,
      for garnish

Sprinkle chicken with salt, pepper and cinnamon; coat lightly with flour, shaking off excess. Brown on both sides in heated oil in a large heavy frying pan. Top with onions, garlic, tomatoes and their liquid, chiles, cumin seed and cloves. Bring to boiling, reduce heat, cover and simmer over low heat until chicken is tender, about 45 minutes. Remove chicken pieces to a warm serving dish, and keep warm. Bring vegetables and cooking liquid to boiling and cook, stirring, over high heat, until sauce is thickened. Pour over chicken. Sprinkle with green onions. Makes 4 servings.

An Ancient Implement

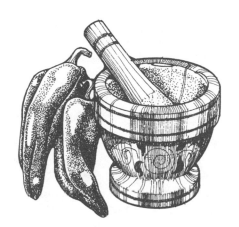

There is a place in today's kitchen for an attractive implement that wouldn't have been out of place in an alchemist's laboratory in the Middle Ages—a mortar and pestle. Mexican cooking brings many of its functions into play: crushing cumin, sesame or anise seeds to release their flavors, breaking up the coarse skin and seeds of a dried chile, bruising saffron threads.

Because it is necessary to wash the mortar (the container) and the pestle (the part that does the pounding and crushing) after each use to remove the flavor of clinging oils, a heavy porcelain, stoneware or glass set will be more functional than wood. Look for a mortar and pestle in gourmet cookware shops, or in a supply house for chemists and pharmacists.

Chicken in Creamy Almond Sauce   *(Pollo Almendrado)*

Using finely ground nuts or seeds to flavor and thicken a sauce is characteristic of Mexican cooking. In this recipe, ground almonds add substance to a delicately seasoned cream sauce and simmered chicken.

3   pounds meaty chicken pieces
    Salt
½   cup ground unblanched almonds
       (whirl in food processor or
       blender until powdery)
2   tablespoons butter or margarine
1   tablespoon salad oil
1   medium onion, finely chopped
1   clove garlic, minced or pressed
1   large tomato, peeled and chopped
½   cup *each* regular-strength chicken
       broth (homemade or canned)
       and whipping cream
    Sliced green onions, for garnish
       (use part of tops)

Sprinkle chicken with salt. Coat well with almonds. Brown on all sides in mixture of butter and oil in a large deep frying pan over medium heat. Spoon off excess fat, if necessary. Top chicken with onion, garlic, tomato and any remaining ground almonds. Pour on broth. Bring to boiling, cover, reduce heat and simmer slowly until chicken is very tender, 45 minutes to 1 hour. Remove chicken to a warm deep platter. Add cream to cooking liquid and bring it to boiling; cook and stir until sauce is reduced and thickened. Salt to taste; pour sauce over chicken. Sprinkle with sliced green onions. Accompany with rice and a green vegetable. Makes 4 to 6 servings.

A *pipian* is a sauce thickened with some sort of seeds—such as pumpkin seed kernels or sesame seeds. Sesame seeds are used in this well seasoned chicken simmered in tomato sauce. Toasting brings out the nutlike flavor.

Chicken in Red Sesame Sauce   *(Pollo en Pipian Colorado)*

¼ cup toasted sesame seeds
   (directions follow)
1 small dried red pepper, coarsely
   chopped
6 chicken legs with thighs
   attached (about 3 lbs.)
2 tablespoons lard
1 large onion, finely chopped
2 cloves garlic, minced or pressed
1 can (1 lb.) tomatoes, coarsely
   chopped
1 tablespoon tomato paste
1 can (4 oz.) green chiles, seeded
   and chopped
1 tablespoon chile powder
1 teaspoon salt
½ teaspoon *each* ground cinnamon
   and coriander
¼ teaspoon *each* ground cloves
   and crushed anise seeds

In a small blender jar whirl together sesame seeds and dried red pepper until powdery. Brown chicken legs on all sides, three or four at a time, in heated lard in a large heavy frying pan or electric skillet. Spoon off excess fat. Add onion, garlic, tomatoes and their liquid, tomato paste, ground sesame seed mixture, green chiles, chile powder, salt and spices. Bring to boiling, cover, reduce heat and simmer for about 1 hour, until chicken is very tender. Remove chicken to a warm platter. Bring sauce to boiling and cook, stirring frequently, until sauce is reduced and thickened. Salt to taste. Pour sauce over chicken. Serve with rice. Makes 6 servings.

To toast sesame seeds: Spread in a shallow pan. Bake in a 350° oven, stirring occasionally, until golden brown, 8 to 10 minutes.

Simply cooked chicken is popular in Mexico, too. After marinating it in oil, lime or lemon juice and a generous quantity of oregano, chicken quarters can be broiled or barbecued.

Broiled Chicken with Oregano *(Pollo con Orégano)*

1 frying chicken (2½ to 3 lbs.),
   quartered
⅓ cup salad oil
1½ tablespoons lime or lemon juice
1 teaspoon salt
1 tablespoon crumbled oregano
2 cloves garlic, minced or pressed
   Tomato slices and chopped
    green onions, for garnish

Place chicken quarters in a shallow glass or enamel baking dish. In a covered jar, shake together oil, lime or lemon juice, salt, oregano and garlic until well combined. Pour over chicken. Cover and chill for 3 to 4 hours or overnight, turning and stirring marinade occasionally. Drain chicken, reserving marinade. Broil 6 to 8 inches from heat (or barbecue over low coals) for 12 to 15 minutes on each side, until chicken is completely cooked in the thickest part (test with a small sharp knife). While cooking, brush several times with reserved marinade. Garnish with tomato slices sprinkled with green onions. Accompany with Green Beans and Carrots with Cumin Sautéed Onions (see page 93). Makes 4 servings.

Marinated Chicken en Brochette *(Brocheta de Pollo Marinada)*

Brochettes of boneless chicken marinated in, then flamed with, tequila make a dramatic company dish from the broiler or barbecue grill.

3 whole chicken breasts (6 halves,
   about 3 lbs.), boned and
   skinned
   Juice of 1 lime (about 2½ tbsp.)
2 tablespoons salad oil
1 teaspoon salt
½ teaspoon oregano
¼ teaspoon ground cumin
1 small dried red pepper, crushed
6 tablespoons tequila
1 green bell pepper, seeded and
   cut in 1-inch squares
½ medium onion, separated into
   layers and cut in 1-inch squares
   Radish roses and green onions,
    for garnish

Cut boned chicken into 1-1/2-inch squares. Place in a shallow glass bowl and pour on a mixture of lime juice, oil, seasonings and 4 tablespoons of the tequila; stir to coat well. Cover and refrigerate for 1 to 3 hours. Thread chicken pieces on 6 metal skewers, alternating them with green pepper and onion squares; reserve marinade. Broil about 6 inches from heat, or barbecue over a low fire, until chicken is cooked in the thickest part (insert a small sharp knife to check) and lightly browned, 10 to 15 minutes on each side. Transfer to a heatproof platter, and keep warm. Bring marinade to boiling and reduce it by about half. Pour over chicken. Heat remaining 2 tablespoons tequila just until lukewarm. Ignite and drizzle, flaming, over chicken. Serve immediately, garnished with radish roses and green onions. Accompany with Guacamole (see page 15) and Baked Rice with Cheese (see page 96). Makes 6 servings.

Learn to Bone Chicken Breasts

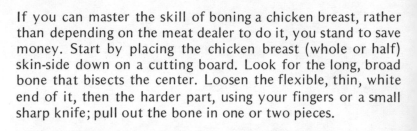

If you can master the skill of boning a chicken breast, rather than depending on the meat dealer to do it, you stand to save money. Start by placing the chicken breast (whole or half) skin-side down on a cutting board. Look for the long, broad bone that bisects the center. Loosen the flexible, thin, white end of it, then the harder part, using your fingers or a small sharp knife; pull out the bone in one or two pieces.

Then, for each half breast, insert tip of knife under the long rib bone. Work the knife underneath the bone and cut it away from the meat—pull up on the bones and push and scrape the meat downward and free. Keep cutting around the outer edge of the breast to and then through the shoulder joint to remove the entire rib cage.

Working from the ends, scrape meat away from each side of the wishbone; cut and lift it out. Turn the meat over and pull away the skin with your fingers. Reserve the bones and skin to make chicken broth.

Although it generally appears on restaurant menus as a first course, this soup seems better suited to serving as a main dish. It is so full of flavor, color and fresh healthy ingredients that it deserves full meal status. The avocado should be added just as the soup is served.

Chicken and Avocado Soup *(Caldo Tlalpeño)*

1	large frying or stewing chicken (about 3 lbs.), cut up
1	stalk celery, thinly sliced
2	medium carrots, thinly sliced
2	medium onions, thinly sliced
1	clove garlic, crushed
1	teaspoon salt
½	teaspoon *each* crumbled oregano and dried cumin
1	to 2 small dried red peppers, crushed
1	can (1 lb.) tomatoes
4	cups water
1	medium zucchini, thinly sliced
¼	cup chopped fresh cilantro, *or* 2 teaspoons dried cilantro
2	avocados, peeled and sliced
	Sour cream
	Lime wedges

In a 5 to 6-quart kettle or Dutch oven, combine chicken, celery, carrots, onions, garlic, seasonings (except cilantro), tomatoes (broken up with a fork) and water. Bring to boiling, cover, reduce heat and simmer until chicken is very tender and broth is flavorful, 2 to 2-1/2 hours. Remove chicken pieces; discard bones and skin, and return meat in large chunks to the soup (you can prepare the soup ahead to this point, cover and refrigerate, if you wish). Add zucchini and *dried* cilantro (if you are using it in place of the fresh). Taste and add salt, if needed. Cook for about 5 minutes longer, until chicken is heated through and zucchini is tender-crisp. Stir in fresh cilantro. Top each serving with avocado slices and a dollop of sour cream. Accompany with lime wedges to squeeze into soup to taste. Makes 4 to 5 main dish servings.

Turkey is one of Mexico's contributions to the world's cuisine. When turkeys were brought to Europe from the New World, they were thought quite exotic. In each culture the bird acquired a name indicating a certain confusion about its origin. The French called it *dinde* ("from India"), the Italian word is *tacchino* ("from China"). Back home in Mexico the Aztecs called it *huaxolotl*, a word that has evolved into today's *guajolote*. Turkey is also known in Mexico as *pavo*.

The best known Mexican preparation of turkey is *mole* (say MOE-*leh*). Actually, there are a number of kinds of sauces known as moles—red ones, green ones and also pale creamy ones. The most familiar is the deep, dark and delicious one that was originally created in the city of Puebla. It includes several kinds of dried chiles, ground nuts and sesame seeds, a variety of spices and most surprisingly of all, chocolate!

I have always wondered if it might be possible to make this sort of mole more accessible and somewhat less tedious to prepare. The following mole is cooked all in one pot, with a generous assist from the blender or food processor. All the ingredients are readily available. And it can be made ahead.

Turkey Mole   *(Mole de Guajolote)*

5   pounds (about) turkey legs and thighs
2   tablespoons lard
2   medium onions, finely chopped
3   cloves garlic, minced or pressed
1   can (1 lb.) tomatoes, coarsely chopped
¼   cup tomato paste
1   can (13¾ oz.) regular-strength chicken broth
⅓   cup raisins
½   cup blanched almonds
¼   cup toasted sesame seeds (directions follow)
2   small dried red peppers
2   tablespoons chile powder
1   teaspoon salt
½   teaspoon *each* ground cinnamon and coriander
¼   teaspoon *each* ground cloves and crushed anise seeds
1   ounce (1 square) unsweetened chocolate, chopped

In a 5 to 6-quart Dutch oven, brown two or three turkey legs and thighs at a time well on all sides in heated lard; return all to pan. Mix in onions, garlic, tomatoes and their liquid, tomato paste, chicken broth and raisins. In a food processor or blender combine almonds, 3 tablespoons of the sesame seeds and the dried red peppers; whirl together until powdery. Add almond mixture to turkey, together with the chile powder, salt, cinnamon, coriander, cloves and anise seeds. Bring mixture to boiling, cover, reduce heat and simmer for 3 to 4 hours, until turkey is very tender. Use a slotted spoon to remove turkey pieces.

When turkey is cool enough to handle, remove and discard skin, tendons and bones. Divide turkey into large pieces. Bring sauce to boiling and cook, stirring occasionally, until reduced and thickened, 10 to 15 minutes. Whirl about half of the sauce at a time in a food processor or blender until smooth. Return all of the sauce to the cooking pan; mix in chocolate until melted and well combined. Salt to taste. Return turkey to sauce (this much can be done ahead, covered and refrigerated). Cover and simmer for 30 minutes. Sprinkle with remaining 1 tablespoon whole toasted sesame seeds. Serve with rice. Makes 6 to 8 servings.

To toast sesame seeds: Spread in a shallow pan. Heat in a 350° oven, stirring occasionally, for about 10 minutes.

FISH & SHELLFISH

David B. Redmond

Mexico's extensive coastlines on both the Gulf and Pacific assure all parts of the country an abundance of fish and shellfish. Even in inland centers such as Mexico City, Guadalajara and Oaxaca, one can find all manner of impeccably fresh seafood, prepared to local preferences.

The most famous preparation of the splendid red snapper from the Gulf is in the style of Veracruz—with a flamboyant tomato sauce.

The red snapper caught in the Gulf of Mexico is not the same fish as that which is sold by that name on the Pacific Coast of the United States. The latter is a common rockfish with a less distinctive flavor. Fillets of the two can be used interchangeably, but those who can obtain the genuine article will have the better of it.

Red Snapper, Veracruz Style *(Huachinango a la Veracruzana)*

2 medium onions, thinly sliced and separated into rings
3 tablespoons olive oil or salad oil
1 green pepper, quartered, seeded and cut crosswise into thin strips
2 cloves garlic, minced or pressed
1 can (1 lb.) tomatoes, broken up with a fork
   Juice of 1 orange
⅓ cup halved green olives
1 tablespoon drained capers
1 teaspoon salt
½ teaspoon *each* crumbled oregano and ground cumin
1 bay leaf
2 tablespoons chopped fresh cilantro, *or* 1 teaspoon dried cilantro
1 small dried red pepper, crushed
1 small can (4 oz.) pimientos, seeded and cut in strips
2 pounds red snapper fillets, about ½ inch thick (4 to 6 large fillets)
   Salt, pepper and flour
1 tablespoon butter or margarine
   Chopped fresh cilantro or parsley, for garnish

Sauté onion rings in 2 tablespoons of the heated oil in a large heavy saucepan until soft but not browned; stir in green pepper and garlic to coat with oil. Add tomatoes, orange juice, olives, capers, seasonings and all but 1 tablespoon of the pimientos. Bring to boiling, cover, reduce heat and simmer for 1 hour.

Near the end of the cooking time, sprinkle fish fillets with salt and pepper; coat very lightly with flour, shaking off excess. Heat remaining 1 tablespoon oil with butter in a large frying pan. Quickly brown fish fillets lightly on both sides. Pour on sauce. Cover and steam over medium-low heat for 3 to 5 minutes, until fish separates into flakes when tested with a fork. Remove fish to a warm platter and keep warm. Bring sauce to boiling, stirring, and reduce it until thickened; pour over fish. Sprinkle with chopped cilantro or parsley and reserved pimiento strips. Serve with boiled new potatoes or rice. Makes 4 to 6 servings.

Red snapper combines elegantly with one of Mexico's choicest fruits, the mango. A squeeze of fresh lime juice brings out the subtle flavors in both fruit and fish.

Red Snapper with Mango *(Huachinango a la Gloria)*

2 large red snapper fillets, about
    ½ inch thick (about 1 lb.)
1 tablespoon lime juice
    Salt, white pepper and flour
¼ cup butter or margarine
1 tablespoon salad oil
1 firm-ripe mango, peeled and sliced
    Chopped parsley, for garnish
    Lime wedges

Sprinkle fish fillets with lime juice; let stand for 5 minutes. Sprinkle with salt and white pepper; coat lightly with flour. In a large frying pan over moderate heat combine 2 tablespoons of the butter and salad oil; heat until bubbly. Place prepared fish fillets in butter mixture; cook for 2 to 3 minutes on each side, turning once, until fish is golden brown and separates into flakes when tested with a fork. Remove to a warm platter and keep warm. In a small frying pan, melt remaining 2 tablespoons butter. Turn mango slices in hot butter until heated through. Spoon mango and its cooking liquid over fish. Sprinkle with parsley. Serve immediately with lime wedges. Accompany with fluffy rice and cooked spinach. Makes 2 servings.

The Exotic Mango

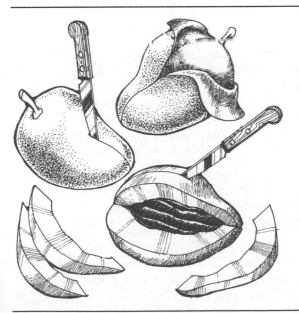

Thanks to increased shipments from Florida, Mexico and the Caribbean, the mango is not as rare in the United States as it once was. This juiciest of all tropical fruits deserves to be better known. Look for mangoes between May and September, when the Florida crop comes to market.

Mangoes are oval in shape and about the size of a large avocado. The color ranges from green through yellow to a sort of sunset pink-orange. For best flavor, choose one that is beginning to take on color, and then let it ripen at room temperature until it begins to soften.

To prepare a mango, cut it around the circumference from end to end as you would an avocado, then peel back the skin banana-style. The seed of a mango is rather large and flat; cut slices of fruit away from the seed as you would a cling peach. A ripe mango is exceedingly juicy, so do this over a bowl or the kitchen sink.

The tart flavor of the little green *tomatillo* is especially complementary to quickly sautéed fish fillets.

Fish Fillets in Tart Green Sauce   *(Pescado en Salsa Verde)*

1   medium onion, chopped
1   clove garlic, minced or pressed
¼   cup (about) olive oil or salad oil
1   cup chopped fresh or drained
      canned *tomatillos* (Mexican
      green tomatoes)
2   canned green chiles, seeded
      and chopped
1   tablespoon lime or lemon juice
¼   cup water or liquid from
      canned tomatillos
2   tablespoons chopped fresh cilan-
      tro, *or* 2 teaspoons dried
      cilantro
1½   pounds small fish fillets, such as
      sole or Pacific ocean perch
      Salt, ground cumin and flour
      Chopped fresh cilantro or pars-
      ley and lime wedges, for garnish

In a saucepan or small frying pan, cook onion and garlic in 1 tablespoon of the oil until soft but not browned; add *tomatillos,* green chiles, lime juice, water and cilantro. Bring to boiling, cover, reduce heat and simmer for about 20 minutes; whirl in blender until smooth. Salt to taste. Reheat sauce to serving temperature.

Sprinkle fish fillets lightly on both sides with salt and cumin. Coat with flour, shaking off excess. Brown lightly on both sides in remaining heated oil in a large frying pan, cooking just until fish is opaque looking and separates readily into flakes when tested with a fork. Remove fish to a warm platter and top with heated sauce. Garnish with chopped cilantro and lime wedges. Makes 6 servings.

Green Tomatoes from Mexico

A vital ingredient in the tart green sauces served with so many Mexican dishes is the *tomatillo* (say *toe-mah*-TEE-*yoh*). Resembling a small green tomato, the tomatillo can be distinguished by its papery light brownish husk. Inside, the flesh is denser and firmer than that of a tomato, and the seeds are much smaller. It's good both raw and cooked. To use fresh tomatillos, remove the husk, wash the fruit inside and cut out the stem.

Tomatillos are available fresh in grocery stores in some Mexican-American neighborhoods. They can also be found in 13 and 14-ounce cans in the Mexican food section of many supermarkets.

Growing your own tomatillos from the seeds of the fresh fruit is also possible. The mature plants attain about the same size as a cherry tomato plant.

Broiled bacon-wrapped shrimp stuffed with cheese is a popular main dish in Guadalajara. You might also serve this as an appetizer at a stand-up party.

Broiled Shrimp with Cheese and Bacon   *(Camarones Rellenos de Queso con Tocino)*

1 pound (25 to 30) large shrimp
   in shells
2 tablespoons salad oil
1 tablespoon lime or lemon juice
1 clove garlic, minced or pressed
¼ teaspoon crumbled oregano
4 ounces Monterey jack cheese,
   cut in 25 to 30 strips, ¾-inch
   long and ¼-inch thick
  Sliced bacon (13 to 15 strips),
   cut in half crosswise
  Tomato wedges and cilantro or
   parsley sprigs

Shell and devein shrimp. Using a small sharp knife, cut an inch-long slit in the thicker end of each shrimp, cutting almost to the underside. Shake or whirl together in a small blender jar the oil, lime or lemon juice, garlic and oregano. Place prepared shrimp in a bowl, pour on oil mixture, mix lightly to coat shrimp well, cover and refrigerate for 1 to 3 hours. Remove shrimp from marinade.

Place a strip of cheese in pocket in each shrimp. Partially cook bacon slices until they begin to brown; drain on paper towels. Wrap a bacon slice around each shrimp to enclose cheese; fasten with wooden picks. Place bacon-wrapped stuffed shrimp on a rack in broiling pan. Broil, about 6 inches from heat source, until bacon is well browned and shrimp are pink, turning once, a total of 8 to 10 minutes. Garnish with tomato wedges and cilantro or parsley. Serve immediately. Makes 4 servings.

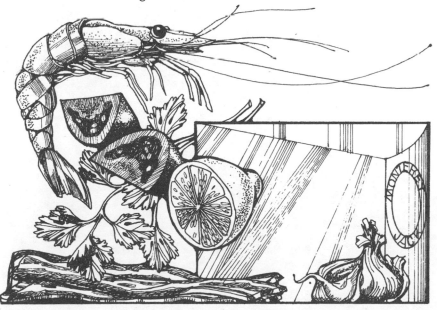

Frozen langostinos from Latin America have been making their way into the U.S. in a handy peeled, cooked form. As such they need little preparation. Reheating them under the broiler in this Mexican-style garlic butter makes a quick main dish to serve with rice and a green salad.

Langostinos Broiled in Garlic Butter   *(Langostinos en Parrilla con Mojo de Ajo)*

½ cup (¼ lb.) soft butter or mar-
    garine
1   tablespoon fresh lime or lemon juice
    Dash cayenne
3   cloves garlic, minced or pressed
1   pound frozen peeled langostinos,
    thawed
    Chopped parsley, for garnish

Mix butter, lime juice, cayenne and garlic until smooth and well combined. Cover and chill for 2 to 3 hours (or longer) to blend flavors; before using, let the butter mixture stand at room temperature for about 30 minutes. Arrange langostinos in a single layer in a shallow baking pan just large enough to hold them all. Dot with butter mixture. Place pan about 6 inches from heat source. Broil, stirring occasionally, until langostinos are beginning to brown lightly and butter is bubbly, 10 to 12 minutes. Sprinkle with chopped parsley. Serve with fluffy rice. Makes 3 to 4 servings.

VEGETABLES & SIDE DISHES TO ENHANCE MEXICAN MEALS

An enchilada or taco is almost unthinkable without refried beans and rice sharing the plate. Sadly, most Mexican restaurants in the United States don't seem to devote as much skill to these side dishes as they should. Sample their counterparts made at home, beginning with the basic ingredients, and see how much better they can be!

When you prepare refried beans, you can start with any one of four varieties—red, pink, pinto or black. The black beans are popular in Yucatán and in Oaxaca. Remember, if you cook more than your family can eat for one meal, refried beans freeze well.

Refried Beans   *(Frijoles Refritos)*

1   cup dried red, pink, pinto or black
        beans
3   cups water
1   medium onion, chopped
1   small dried red pepper, crushed
½   teaspoon salt
3   tablespoons bacon drippings or
        lard
1   clove garlic, minced or pressed
        Shredded Cheddar or Monterey jack
        cheese

Rinse and drain beans; place in a bowl, add water and let stand overnight (or, if you prefer, bring beans and water to boiling in a 2-quart saucepan, boil briskly for 2 minutes, then remove from heat and let stand, covered, for 1 hour). Add onion, red pepper and salt. Bring to boiling, cover, reduce heat and simmer slowly until beans are very tender, about 2-1/2 hours. Using a potato masher, partially mash the beans (this much can be done ahead covered and refrigerated).

To serve, heat drippings or lard in a large frying pan. Add garlic and cooked beans. Cook over medium heat, stirring frequently, until fat is absorbed and beans are heated through, 3 to 5 minutes. Taste and add salt, if needed. Serve topped with shredded cheese. Makes 4 servings (about 2-1/2 cups).

A Guide to Dried Beans

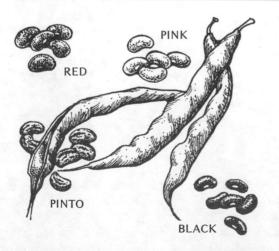

Here are some of the delicious kinds of dried beans used in Mexican cooking. Look for them in bulk bins in health food stores and grocery stores featuring Mexican foods. Or, find them in convenient packages at your local supermarket.

Fresh beans can be pleasant with a Mexican meal, too. You will enjoy them cooked with carrot strips and seasoned with buttery onions sautéed with cumin. It's a colorful vegetable that tastes good with simply cooked meats.

Green Beans and Carrots with Cumin Sautéed Onions

1 medium onion, thinly sliced and
    separated into rings
2 tablespoons butter or margarine
½ teaspoon ground cumin
1 pound green beans, cut in long
    thin strips
1 medium carrot, cut in thin,
    2-inch-long strips
    Boiling salted water

Add onion to heated butter; stir in cumin. Cook slowly, stirring frequently, until onion rings are limp and lightly browned. Meanwhile, cook beans and carrot strips in boiling salted water until tender-crisp, 8 to 10 minutes; drain well. Add onion mixture, mixing lightly. Salt to taste. Makes 4 to 6 servings.

Pickled Carrot Relish *(Zanhorias en Escabeche)*

Sometimes when one sits down in a modest Mexican restaurant, one finds already on the table an innocent looking dish of carrots and onions with a few pale chiles. Don't assume the concoction is as unassuming as pickle relish. The little yellow wax chiles in the mixture can be quite hot, and the longer they share the same container, the more of this hot taste permeates the other vegetables.

It Is a simple mixture to prepare if you have access to the fresh yellow chiles, and it will keep well in the refrigerator for up to a month. Serve it with grilled or barbecued chicken or beef.

1 cup cider vinegar
⅓ cup sugar
2 tablespoons olive oil
1 teaspoon *each* salt and crumbled
    oregano
½ teaspoon whole coriander seeds
1 tablespoon mixed pickling spices,
    tied in a square of cheesecloth
6 medium carrots, sliced about ⅛ inch
2 medium onions, thinly sliced and
    separated into rings
2 cloves garlic, minced or pressed
8 small whole yellow wax chile
    peppers

In a 3-quart saucepan bring to boiling vinegar, sugar, oil, salt, oregano, coriander seeds and bag of pickling spices; stir to dissolve sugar. Cover and simmer for 10 minutes to blend flavors. Add carrots, onions, garlic and chiles. Bring again to boiling, reduce heat, cover and boil gently for about 10 minutes, until carrots are tender-crisp. Discard packet of pickling spices. Transfer carrot mixture to screw-top jars and refrigerate for 2 to 3 days to blend flavors. Serve as a relish with broiled, grilled or roast meats. Keep refrigerated when not in use, and use within 4 weeks. Makes about 1 quart.

One vegetable dish that can very well be a main course is *chiles rellenos* (say CHEE-*lehs* reh-YAY—*nohs*). In the United States the batter-dipped long green chiles are usually filled with melted cheese, but in Mexico they may have a meatier filling. Here are two versions—one with cheese, and the other with a piquant chicken mixture called a *piccadillo* (say *peek-ah*-DEE-*yo*).

Cheese-Stuffed Fresh Green Chiles   *(Chiles Rellenos)*

6   fresh California (Anaheim) green
     chile peppers, prepared as
     directed (directions follow)
6   ounces Monterey jack cheese, cut
     in six 4-inch-long strips
     Flour
5   eggs, separated
¼   teaspoon cream of tartar
½   teaspoon salt
¼   cup flour
     Salad oil for frying

Fill each prepared green chile with a strip of cheese; coat peppers lightly with flour, shaking off excess. For batter, beat egg whites with cream of tartar and salt until soft peaks form. In another bowl (using the same beaters), beat egg yolks until thick; blend in the 1/4 cup flour. Fold egg yolk mixture into beaten egg whites.

Pour oil to a depth of about 1/2 inch into a heavy frying pan or electric skillet. Heat the oil to a temperature of 365°. Coat filled peppers generously with the egg batter, using your hands to coat them completely. Fry peppers, about three at a time, until golden brown on both sides, turning once. Remove with a slotted spatula; drain, and serve immediately. Makes 6 servings.

How To Prepare Fresh Green Chiles

Rinse chiles well, leaving stems on. Place close together on the rack of a broiler pan. Place chiles 2 to 3 inches from heat source. Broil, turning frequently with tongs, until chiles are blistered on all sides. (You can also place rinsed chiles over a low gas flame, turning frequently until lightly browned and blistered.) As each chile is removed from heat, place it immediately into a plastic bag. When all the chiles are in the bag, twist top to enclose the steam and let stand until chiles are cool enough to handle.

Remove each chile from the bag and use a small sharp knife to pull off the paper-like skin. Be careful not to tear the chile. Cut a slit in one side to within 1/4 inch of stem end. Gently remove seeds and pith inside. Rinse and drain before filling with cheese or other stuffing.

If done ahead, place in a covered bowl in the refrigerator until ready to use (as long as overnight).

Fresh Green Chiles Stuffed with Chicken   *(Chiles Rellenos de Picadillo)*

2   half chicken breasts
⅓   cup finely chopped onion
1   clove garlic, minced or pressed
2   tablespoons raisins
½   teaspoon *each* salt and ground
        cinnamon
⅛   teaspoon ground cloves
1   can (8 oz.) tomato sauce
1   tablespoon cider vinegar
¼   cup slivered almonds or toasted
        pine nuts
6   fresh California (Anaheim) green
        or red chile peppers, prepared
        as directed on facing page
      Flour
5   eggs, separated
¼   teaspoon cream of tartar
½   teaspoon salt
¼   cup flour
      Salad oil for frying

Place chicken breasts in a frying pan with onion, garlic, raisins, salt, cinnamon, cloves and tomato sauce. Bring to boiling, cover, reduce heat and simmer for about 45 minutes, until chicken is very tender. Remove and discard chicken bones and skin, shred chicken, and return it to sauce. Cook, stirring occasionally, until filling is thick. Mix in vinegar and nuts. (If you wish, this can be made ahead and refrigerated.) Divide the filling evenly among the prepared green chiles.

Coat filled peppers lightly with flour, shaking off excess. For batter, beat egg whites with cream of tartar and salt until soft peaks form. In another bowl (using the same beaters), beat egg yolks until thick; blend in the 1/4 cup flour. Fold egg yolk mixture into beaten egg whites.

Pour oil to a depth of about 1/2 inch into a heavy frying pan or electric skillet. Heat the oil to a temperature of 365°. Coat filled peppers generously with the egg batter, using your hands to coat them completely. Fry peppers, about three at a time, until golden brown on both sides, turning once. Remove with a slotted spatula; drain, and serve immediately. Makes 6 servings.

Baked Cheese-Stuffed Green Chiles   *(Chiles Rellenos al Horno)*

Making chiles rellenos in the traditional manner, though rewarding, is time consuming—and fresh chiles aren't always available. Lyn Ortega, who teaches the cooking of New Mexico in Albuquerque, has found a way to prepare the dish as a casserole. This recipe specifies canned green chiles, but you can also use six to eight fresh ones, prepared as described on facing page, if you wish.

2   small cans (4 oz. *each*) green chiles
½   pound Monterey jack cheese
1   small onion, finely chopped, sautéed
        until tender in 1 tablespoon
        butter or margarine
4   eggs, separated
⅛   teaspoon cream of tartar
½   teaspoon salt
2   tablespoons flour

Slit each chile lengthwise and carefully remove seeds. Cut cheese into as many strips as there are chiles. Fill chiles with cheese strips; reshape chiles to cover cheese. Place in a single layer in a greased baking pan or shallow casserole (about 2-quart capacity). Sprinkle with sautéed onion. Beat egg whites with cream of tartar and salt until soft peaks form. In another bowl (using the same beaters), beat egg yolks until thick; blend in flour. Fold egg yolk mixture into beaten egg whites. Lightly spread batter over stuffed chiles. Bake in a 325° oven for 20 to 30 minutes, until batter is set and top is lightly browned. Serve at once. Makes 4 to 6 servings.

Here is a recipe for baked rice in the Mexican style with more character than most. It's a good accompaniment to tacos and enchiladas, and also for roast or grilled meats.

Baked Red Rice and Cheese

1   cup long grain white rice
2   tablespoons salad oil
1   medium onion, finely chopped
1   clove garlic, minced or pressed
1   can (8 oz.) tomato sauce
1   cup regular-strength chicken broth, canned or homemade
½   teaspoon *each* salt and cumin
    Dash cayenne
½   cup ripe olive wedges
1½ cups shredded Monterey jack cheese

In a deep heavy saucepan stir rice to coat it with heated oil; stir in onion and garlic and cook until onion browns lightly. Mix in tomato sauce, broth, salt, cumin and cayenne. Bring to boiling, reduce heat and cover tightly. Cook until rice is almost tender, 20 to 22 minutes. Mix in olive wedges and 1 cup of the shredded cheese. Turn into a buttered 5 to 6-cup casserole. Sprinkle remaining cheese over the top. Bake, uncovered, in a 375° oven until cheese is melted and lightly browned, about 15 minutes. Makes 4 to 6 servings.

Tostadita Casserole   *(Sopa Seca de Tortilla)*

The so-called "dry soups" or *sopa secas* in Mexico are made with rice, macaroni or tortillas and are usually served as a first course. For most people here, however, they fit better into a meal as an accompaniment to simply prepared meat, chicken or fish. This casserole is made with tostaditas or corn chips, green chiles and three kinds of cheese.

Tostaditas made from 10 corn tortillas (see page 32), *or*
    1 package (6¼ oz.) tortilla chips
1   large onion, chopped
2   tablespoons butter or margarine
2   eggs
1   cup small curd cottage cheese
¼   teaspoon ground cumin
½   teaspoon salt
    Dash seasoned pepper
1   small can (4 oz.) diced green chiles
3   cups shredded Monterey jack cheese
1   cup sour cream
1   cup shredded Cheddar cheese

Crush enough of the tostaditas or corn chips to make 1/2 cup; set aside. In a skillet, brown onion lightly in butter. In a mixing bowl, beat eggs slightly; add cottage cheese, cumin, salt, pepper and onions. In a buttered shallow 2-quart casserole place half of the uncrushed tostaditas or corn chips. Cover with half *each* of the cottage cheese mixture, green chiles and Monterey jack cheese. Repeat layers, using remaining uncrushed chips, cottage cheese mixture, chiles and jack cheese. Cover casserole and bake in a 350° oven for 25 minutes. Spread with sour cream, then sprinkle with Cheddar cheese and crushed chips. Return to oven and continue baking, uncovered, for 5 to 10 minutes longer, until Cheddar cheese melts. Makes 6 to 8 servings.

Another popular side dish with simply cooked meats is this rice simmered with chicken broth, green chiles, green onions and Monterey jack cheese.

Skillet Green Rice with Chiles *(Arroz Verde)*

1 cup long grain white rice
1 tablespoon *each* salad oil and lard
1 medium onion, finely chopped
1 can (13¾ oz.) regular-strength
     chicken broth
⅓ cup water
½ teaspoon *each* garlic salt and
     ground cumin
1 can (4 oz.) diced green chiles
¼ cup *each* sliced green onions (use
     part of tops) and chopped
     fresh cilantro or parsley
1 cup shredded Monterey jack
     cheese

In a large heavy frying pan with an oven-proof handle, stir rice to coat it with heated oil and lard; stir in onion and cook until it browns lightly. Mix in chicken broth, water, garlic salt, cumin and green chiles. Bring to boiling, reduce heat and cover tightly. Cook until rice is tender, 22 to 25 minutes. Mix in green onions, cilantro and 3/4 cup of the cheese. Sprinkle top with remaining cheese and place under broiler for several seconds until cheese melts. Makes 4 to 6 servings.

Fried bananas add a tropical touch when you include them with Mexican main dishes such as *carne asada*.

Fried Bananas   *(Platanos Fritos)*

4   firm green-tipped bananas
    Lime or lemon juice
    Oil for deep frying
    Flour
    Lime wedges

Peel bananas and cut into diagonal 1/2-inch slices, *or* cut in half crosswise and then lengthwise. If done ahead, rub with lime or lemon juice to prevent darkening. Pour oil to a depth of at least 1/2 inch in a heavy frying pan, electric frying pan or Chinese wok. Heat oil to 350° to 375°. Coat bananas lightly with flour; fry, about 6 at a time, until lightly browned, 1 to 2 minutes. Drain on paper towels. Keep warm in a pan in a 250° oven until all are fried. Serve with lime wedges to squeeze over bananas. Makes 4 servings.

Lime Glazed Papaya Wedges

A very quick accompaniment for broiled or barbecued chicken is tart-sweet papaya. Be sure the papaya you choose is at least partly golden—the more the better. Let it ripen at room temperature until no green color remains, but use it before it begins to show blotchy dark spots.

1   firm-ripe papaya (1¼ to 1½ lbs.)
2   tablespoons *each* butter or
        margarine and brown sugar
    Juice of 1 lime
    Dash cinnamon

Peel papaya and cut it in half. Scoop out seeds. Cut each half into 6 to 8 long wedges. Heat together butter, brown sugar, lime juice and cinnamon in a medium-sized frying pan over moderate heat until sugar is dissolved and mixture bubbles. Place papaya slices in hot syrup and heat, spooning syrup over, until papaya is glazed and warmed through. Serve immediately. Makes 4 servings.

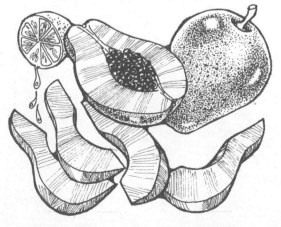

BREAD · ART FROM THE OVEN

David B. Redmond

Baking bread is surely one of the most creative kinds of cooking. The breads of Mexico are so notable in their diversity and imagination that it is especially satisfying to make them at home. Like most yeast breads they freeze well, so any surplus can be tucked away for a future treat.

The crusty rolls called *bolillos* (say *bow*-LEE-*yohs*) can be enjoyed at any meal. Try them split and toasted at breakfast, for heroically proportioned sandwiches at lunch, or sliced as warm, miniature loaves at dinner.

Crusty Mexican Rolls   *(Bolillos)*

1   package yeast, active dry or
        compressed
1⅓ cups warm water (lukewarm for
        compressed yeast)
1   tablespoon sugar
2   teaspoons salt
1   tablespoon cooled melted lard
4   cups unsifted all-purpose
        flour (about)
1   teaspoon cornstarch, dissolved
        in ⅓ cup water

Sprinkle yeast over warm water in a large bowl; let stand for 3 to 5 minutes until dissolved. Mix in sugar, salt and lard. Add 2-1/2 cups of the flour; mix to blend and then beat at medium speed of an electric mixer until dough is elastic and pulls away from sides of bowl, about 5 minutes. With a wooden spoon stir in 1 cup more of the flour. Spread remaining 1/2 cup flour on a board or pastry cloth, and turn dough out onto it. Knead until dough is very smooth and elastic and tiny bubbles can be seen just below the surface, 20 to 25 minutes. (Knead in up to 1/4 cup additional flour, if necessary.) Place dough in a greased bowl, turning to grease top. Cover and let rise until almost doubled, about 1 hour. Punch dough down, then turn out onto a lightly floured surface and knead it for a few seconds to release air bubbles. Let rest 10 minutes.

To shape dough, divide it into 10 equal-sized pieces. Knead and roll each into a ball, then use the palms of both hands to roll from either side to taper and elongate the ends (each roll should be about 5-1/2 inches long and 2 inches wide at center). Place shaped rolls on greased or nonstick baking sheets; cover lightly with waxed paper. Let rise until puffy looking, about 25 minutes. While rolls are rising, bring cornstarch mixture to boiling, stirring until thickened and clear. Just before baking, brush rolls lightly with warm cornstarch mixture. Slash each down the center, almost from end to end, using a razor blade or small sharp knife and cutting about 1/2 inch deep. Bake in a 375° oven until crust is golden brown and rolls sound hollow when tapped lightly, 30 to 35 minutes. Cool on wire racks. Makes 10 rolls.

More than one Mexican restaurant has made its reputation by serving hot freshly made *sopaipillas* (say *soap-ah*-PEA-*yahs*) and honey with every meal. These fat little fried triangles or pillows can be made from just about any kind of dough, but using a yeast dough makes them particularly delicious. Here are two versions, one beginning with frozen bread dough, the other starting from scratch.

Quick Sopaipillas

1   loaf (1 lb.) frozen bread dough,
       thawed in refrigerator
    Oil for deep frying
    Powdered sugar, cinnamon sugar
       or honey

Roll dough out on a floured board or pastry cloth to a 9 by 12-inch rectangle. Cut into 3-inch squares, then cut each square in half to make two triangles. Heat oil to 365°. Fry dough, three or four triangles at a time, turning once, until well browned on both sides, 2 to 3 minutes in all. Drain on paper towels. Serve warm, sprinkled with powdered sugar or cinnamon sugar, or with honey to drizzle on at the table. Makes 2 dozen.

Sopaipillas

¾   cup milk
2   tablespoons *each* lard and butter
       or margarine
⅓   cup sugar
1   teaspoon salt
1   package yeast, active dry or
       compressed
¼   cup warm water (lukewarm for
       compressed yeast)
3¾ cups unsifted all-purpose
       flour (about)
1   egg
    Oil for deep frying
    Powdered sugar, cinnamon sugar
       or honey

Heat milk with lard, butter, sugar and salt, stirring until shortening melts and sugar is dissolved. Let milk mixture stand until lukewarm. In a large bowl, soften yeast in warm water. Add cooled milk mixture and 2 cups of the flour; mix to blend, then beat with an electric mixer until smooth and elastic. Add egg, then gradually beat in 1 cup more flour. Using a heavy wooden spoon, stir in about 1/2 cup more flour to make a soft dough. Turn out on a board or pastry cloth floured with as much as 1/4 cup of the remaining flour. Knead until smooth and elastic, 15 to 20 minutes, kneading in just enough flour to keep dough from being too sticky. Place in a greased bowl, cover, and let rise in a warm place until doubled, about 1-1/2 hours. Punch dough down. On a floured board or pastry cloth, roll it to a 12-inch square, about 1/2 inch thick. Cut into 4-inch squares, then cut each square in half to make two triangles. Pull the triangles apart to separate them, then let them rise on the board for about 30 minutes.

Meanwhile, heat oil to a depth of at least 2 inches in a heavy frying pan, electric skillet or Chinese wok to 365°. Fry *sopaipillas*, three or four at a time, turning once, until well browned on both sides, 2-1/2 to 3 minutes in all. Drain and serve warm, sprinkled with powdered sugar or cinnamon sugar, or with honey to drizzle on at the table. Makes 18.

Mexican sweet bread or *pan dulce* (say *pahn* DOOL-*say*) is as much fun to make as it is to eat. Each round puffy roll is topped with a sweet crumbly mixture flavored with cinnamon or vanilla. In this topping you incise a design such as diamonds, a shell or a fanciful snail; or just crumble the topping irregularly. Try some each way!

Mexican Sweet Bread   *(Pan Dulce)*

1   cup warm milk
2   tablespoons *each* butter or margarine and lard
⅓   cup sugar
1   teaspoon salt
2   packages dry yeast, active dry or compressed
¼   cup warm water (lukewarm for compressed yeast)
3   eggs
5½   cups (about) unsifted all-purpose flour
     Sweet Crumbly Topping (recipe follows)

Pour milk over butter and lard, sugar and salt in a large bowl; stir until butter and lard melt. Let stand until cooled to lukewarm. Meanwhile, soften yeast in warm water in a small bowl. To cooled milk mixture add yeast, eggs and 3 cups of the flour. Mix to blend, then beat with electric mixer at medium speed until batter is very smooth and elastic, 3 to 5 minutes. Stir in 2 cups more flour to make a soft dough. Turn out onto a board or pastry cloth floured with some of the remaining 1/2 cup flour. Knead until dough is smooth and small bubbles form just under the surface, 15 to 20 minutes, kneading in just enough additional flour as needed to prevent stickiness. Place in greased bowl, cover and let rise in a warm place until doubled, 45 minutes to 1 hour. Punch dough down.

Divide dough into 12 equal portions; shape each into a round ball and place well apart on greased or nonstick baking sheets. Cover with Sweet Crumbly Cinnamon or Vanilla Topping as directed below. Let rise until rolls are puffy and almost doubled in bulk, about 30 minutes. Bake in a 375° oven for about 20 minutes, until well browned. Makes 12 large rolls.

Sweet Crumbly Cinnamon or Vanilla Topping: In a bowl mix 1/2 cup sugar, 1 teaspoon cinnamon (if used) and 3/4 cup unsifted all-purpose flour. Cut in 1/4 cup firm butter or margarine with a pastry blender until fine even crumbs form. With a fork stir in 1 teaspoon vanilla (if used) and 1 egg yolk until well blended. Press mixture together with your hands to form a ball, then divide it into 12 equal portions.

For each *crumble-topped* roll, break 1 portion of the mixture into irregular lumps and arrange in the center, pressing mixture lightly into dough.

To make a *snail or caracol* design, flatten a portion of the topping with a rolling pin on a floured surface, rolling it to about a 3-inch circle. Place over the roll, then use a small sharp knife or razor blade to trace a continuous spiralling circle in the topping, beginning in the middle.

For a *crisscross or diamond* design, roll out topping as above, place atop roll, and make parallel cuts about 1/2 inch apart in both directions.

For a *shell or concha* pattern, roll out topping as above, place atop roll, and cut, beginning in the center of the top edge, in curved parallel lines from top to bottom, making lines farther apart at bottom to resemble a scallop shell.

One of the specialties of the Saturday market in Oaxaca is a sweet egg rich bread made in fat round loaves and flavored with anise seeds. It is called *pan de yema* (say *pahn deh* YAY-*mah*), which simply means egg yolk bread. The name falls far short of describing the bread's sophisticated flavor.

Oaxacan Anise Flavored Egg Bread   *(Pan de Yema)*

1	cup milk
⅔	cup sugar
1½	teaspoons salt
2	packages yeast, active dry or compressed
½	cup warm water (lukewarm for compressed yeast)
5½	cups unsifted, regular all-purpose flour (about)
¼	cup *each* butter or margarine and lard, melted and cooled
3	egg yolks
1	teaspoon anise seeds, crushed
1	egg white, beaten with 1 tablespoon water (for glaze)
	Sesame seeds

Heat milk and pour over sugar and salt in a large bowl. Stir until sugar dissolves and let cool to lukewarm. Soften yeast in warm water; blend into cooled milk mixture. At medium speed of an electric mixer, beat in 2-1/2 cups of the flour to make a smooth batter; cover and let stand in a warm place for 20 minutes until bubbly. Add cooled melted butter and lard mixture, egg yolks and crushed anise seeds. Mix in 1-1/2 cups more flour, then beat until smooth and elastic. Stir in 1 cup more flour to make a soft dough. Turn dough out onto a board or pastry cloth floured generously with the remaining flour; knead until smooth and satiny, 20 to 25 minutes, adding flour only as much as necessary to prevent dough from being too sticky. Place dough in a greased bowl, turning to grease top. Cover; let rise in a warm place until doubled, about 1 hour.

Punch dough down and divide into two equal portions. Shape each into a ball and place on buttered baking sheets. Cover with inverted bowls and let rise until almost doubled, about 45 minutes. Brush lightly with beaten egg white mixture. Using a razor blade or small sharp knife, cut a slash about 1/2 inch deep through the center, from side to side. Sprinkle sesame seeds lightly over top on either side of slash. Bake in a 375° oven for 20 to 25 minutes, until loaves are well browned and a long wooden pick inserted near center comes out clean. Cool on wire racks. Serve warm or at room temperature. Makes 2 loaves.

Many Mexican breads and pastries are made in fanciful shapes, transforming bakery counters into stylized menageries. This example from Oaxaca is intended to resemble a fat turtle. But if you look at the loaves sideways or upside-down, perhaps you can visualize other possibilities. In any event, the bread is delicious!

Oaxacan Turtle-Shaped Loaves   *(Tortugas)*

2 packages yeast, active dry or
    compressed
½ cup warm water (lukewarm for
    compressed yeast)
1¾ cups warm milk
2 tablespoons sugar
2 teaspoons salt
⅓ cup lard, melted and cooled
6 cups unsifted all-purpose flour
    (about)

Dissolve yeast in warm water in a large bowl. Stir in warm milk, sugar, salt and 3 tablespoons of the melted lard. Add 2 cups of the flour and beat at medium speed of an electric mixer for 2 minutes; stir in 2 cups more flour and beat for 5 minutes longer, until dough is very elastic. Using a heavy wooden spoon, stir in 1-1/2 cups more flour to make a stiff dough. Turn dough out on a well floured board or pastry cloth and knead in enough additional flour, about 1/2 cup, to make a smooth elastic dough (this will require 15 to 20 minutes' kneading). Place in a greased bowl, turning to coat top of dough. Cover and let rise in a warm place until doubled, 45 minutes to 1 hour. Punch down; cover dough with a bowl on floured surface and let rest for 10 minutes.

To shape dough, divide it into two equal parts. On a floured surface pat or roll each portion into a rectangle with well rounded corners, about 12 inches long and 8 inches wide. Place on greased baking sheets. Brush top with some of the remaining melted lard. Fold not quite in half, so the underneath edge extends 1/2 inch beyond the top edge. Then twist each corner of the folded edge completely around to form a knob; tuck it underneath to hold it in place. Cover shaped loaves lightly with waxed paper and let rise until nearly doubled, about 45 minutes.

Bake loaves in a 375° oven until well browned, 25 to 30 minutes. As soon as you take the loaves from the oven, brush them lightly with remaining melted lard. Let cool on wire racks. Makes 2 loaves.

Accessories to Improve Your Bread Baking

When you bake Mexican-style breads, you will use the same tools you use for making any other kind of yeast bread. Here are some accessories all good bread bakers will find helpful— or just fun to use.

Baking sheets with nonstick coatings do not need to be greased, even for baking breads coated with egg white or other sticky glazes. Look for sturdy baking sheets that won't warp when placed in a hot oven. The darker the baking sheet or bread pan, the crisper the bread crust will be.

For applying glazes, use a soft, light pastry brush that will not tear the unbaked dough. Some bakers prefer a delicate goose-feather brush (many gourmet shops sell them) for this very reason.

A single-edged razor blade works well for cutting decorative slashes or other designs in the top of long or round loaves of bread or rolls just before baking. You can also use one of the precise, small bladed knives sold in art supply stores.

To keep the crisp crust that is so desirable in homemade yeast bread, transfer loaves from baking sheets to wire cooling racks as soon as possible. Be sure you have several good sized cooling racks ready for this purpose.

A long bladed serrated knife is best for slicing baked breads.

DESSERTS WITH MEXICAN FLAIR

David B. Redmond

Mexico's wonderful fruits such as limes, bananas and pineapples mean that the dessert at the end of a special dinner is truly something to anticipate. An abundance of such luscious ingredients as nuts, coconut, chocolate, vanilla and spices, not to mention rum and coffee, also gives pastry and dessert chefs plenty of inspiration.

A spectacular dessert to prepare at the table is flaming bananas with rum, crème de cacao and brandy. Serve the bananas over vanilla or coffee ice cream. For convenience, have the ice cream all scooped into dessert dishes and waiting in the freezer.

Guadalajaran Bananas Flambé

¼ cup butter or margarine
¼ cup firmly packed brown sugar
   Juice of 1 orange (about ⅔ cup)
1½ tablespoons lime juice
4 firm bananas
2 tablespoons *each* dark rum and
      crème de cacao
¼ cup brandy
   Ice cream

In a chafing dish over an alcohol flame or in a cook-and-serve frying pan, melt butter over medium heat. Stir in brown sugar, orange juice and lime juice; cook, stirring occasionally, until mixture is thick and bubbling and sugar is dissolved and syrupy. Meanwhile, peel bananas and slice them diagonally about 1/2 inch thick. Add to butter and sugar mixture, stirring to coat well. Lightly mix in rum and crème de cacao. Warm brandy slightly in a small metal pan; add to banana mixture, ignite, stir briefly, then spoon flaming bananas over ice cream in individual dishes. Makes 4 servings.

Pyromania at the Dinner Table

For festive occasions a flaming dessert is always impressive. To be sure your special occasion is as dramatic as it deserves to be, follow these tips. Brandy or other liqueurs with a fairly high alcohol content flame most readily. Look at the listed "proof" on the label. A 100-proof brandy is 50 percent alcohol and flames very easily. Liqueurs below about 75 proof are more difficult to ignite. It's the alcohol that burns, and after it is spent what remains is the flavor of the other ingredients.

Brandies and liqueurs will ignite more readily if they are warmed slightly—just until they feel barely warm to the touch. Heating them too much will drive off the alcohol as vapor, leaving nothing to burn. *Always* transfer the required amount of flammable liquid to a separate container to warm and ignite; pouring it directly from a bottle near an open flame can be very dangerous.

Ignite the brandy or other liqueur with a match, or by tipping the pan to catch the flame of a gas range or chafing dish. For greater drama, present the flaming dish in a somewhat darkened room; alcohol burns with a soft blue flame that may be difficult to distinguish under bright lights.

A ubiquitous entry on every Mexican dessert menu is *flan* (say *flahn*), or custard, in some form. This one combines orange, caramel and coffee flavors.

Coffee Caramel Orange Custard   *(Flan al Kahlua)*

⅓ cup sugar
6 eggs
2 tablespoons coffee flavored
      liqueur, such as Kahlua
      or Tia Maria
3 tablespoons honey
1¾ cups milk
½ teaspoon grated orange rind

Melt the sugar in a 9-inch pie pan over moderately high heat, holding pan with potholders and tipping and tilting it so sugar caramelizes evenly and coats sides and bottom of the pan. Set aside to cool and harden. Beat together eggs, coffee liqueur and honey, then gradually mix in milk and orange rind. Pour into caramel-lined pan and place in a larger pan in about 1/2 inch of hot water. Bake at 325° for 35 to 40 minutes, until a knife inserted near center comes out clean. Chill. Loosen edge, then invert custard carefully onto a rimmed serving dish. Cut into wedges, spooning the caramel sauce over each serving. Makes 6 servings.

Mexican Sugar Cookies   *(Polvorones)*

The sugar cookies baked in every part of Mexico are called *polvorones* (say *pole-vohr*-ROH- *nehs*). Using lard as part of the shortening makes them melt-in-your-mouth tender.

½ cup *each* soft butter or margarine
      and lard
¾ cup sugar
1 egg yolk
1 teaspoon vanilla
2½ cups unsifted all-purpose flour
¼ teaspoon cinnamon
    Dash salt
    Sugar

In large bowl of electric mixer cream butter and lard with sugar until fluffy. Beat in egg yolk and vanilla. Sift together flour, cinnamon and salt. Gradually add flour mixture to creamed mixture, beating until well combined. To shape each cooky, make a ball the size of a small walnut, and roll it in sugar to coat generously. Place cookies on greased or non-stick baking sheets. Using a glass dipped in sugar, press each cooky down to about 1/2 inch thickness. Bake in a 275° oven for 20 minutes, then increase heat to 350° and bake for 8 to 10 minutes longer, until lightly browned. Carefully remove to wire racks to cool (hot cookies are fragile). Makes 3 dozen.

Crêpes have become an international favorite. Here is a Mexican version with a caramel and toasted walnut sauce.

Caramel Crêpes with Walnuts   *(Crepas de Cajeta y Nuez)*

Crêpes (recipe follows)
1   cup whipping cream
½   cup firmly packed raw sugar or
      brown sugar
      Cinnamon stick (about 2-inch
      piece)
⅓   cup finely chopped toasted
      walnuts
      Whipped cream

Make crêpes, using a 6-inch pan. In a frying pan over direct heat, an electric frying pan or a crêpes Suzette pan, combine whipping cream, raw or brown sugar and cinnamon stick. Bring to boiling, stirring until sugar is dissolved and cream is reduced by about one-third. Remove cinnamon stick. Reduce heat to low and add crêpes, one by one, turning them with tongs to coat with cream mixture, then folding them in quarters and placing them to one side until all the crêpes are added. Sprinkle with walnuts. Serve with additional whipped cream to spoon over each serving to taste. Makes 4 to 6 servings, 3 crêpes each.

Crêpes: In a food processor or a blender container combine 1 cup unsifted all-purpose flour, 3/4 cup *each* water and milk, 3 eggs, 2 tablespoons *each* sugar and cooled melted butter, a dash of cinnamon and 1/4 teaspoon salt. Whirl for about 1 minute at high speed; scrape down sides with a rubber spatula, then whirl again for about 15 seconds. Cover and refrigerate batter for 1 hour or longer before making crêpes.

Special Cook-at-the Table Ware

Elegant cookware in such precious metals as silver and copper has long been a favorite gift. If you have some of these lovely pieces, don't be shy about using them. With a little practice, you can bring them to the table to make dramatic desserts with all the flair of an accomplished headwaiter.

A chafing dish is perfect for fruit and other dessert sauces. If it's something that takes a long time to cook, you can start it in the kitchen, then reheat it over the chafing dish flame at the table. Arrange last minute ingredients on a tray.

Another very special piece is the large, shallow crêpes Suzette pan. The crêpes are actually made in another pan, and the large shallow crêpes Suzette pan is designed for saucing and serving them. Usually you make the sauce, get it hot and bubbling in the crêpes Suzette pan, then add the crêpes one at a time, coating and folding them with the sauce. The large surface area of the pan accommodates enough crêpes to serve a dinner party. Use the pan over an alcohol burner or your chafing dish burner.

When you plan to cook at the table with one of these special pieces, check the burner several hours before dinner to be sure it has plenty of fuel. Burners that use denatured alcohol should be filled well in advance to allow the fuel to soak in.

The versatile flour tortilla can even turn up as dessert. Here it is made into a puffy, fried burrito with a hot apple filling.

Apple Burritos

3 cups chopped peeled apples
1 tablespoon lime or lemon juice
1 tablespoon water
½ teaspoon cinnamon
½ cup sugar
1 tablespoon flour
   Flour tortillas (recipe follows)
   Oil for deep frying
   Powdered sugar

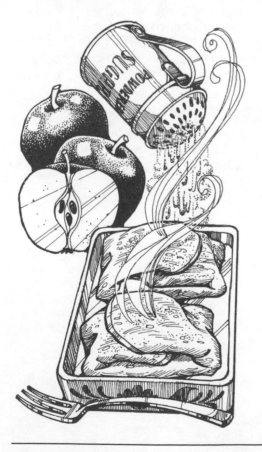

In a 1-1/2-quart saucepan combine apples, lime or lemon juice, water and cinnamon. Bring to boiling over medium heat, cover and simmer, stirring occasionally, until apples are just tender, 6 to 8 minutes. Mix sugar and flour; stir into apples and cook, stirring until thickened. Remove from heat. Place about 1 tablespoon of the apple filling in center of each flour tortilla. Fold in sides, then fold up as for a burrito. Moisten ends to seal. Pour oil to a depth of at least 1 inch in a heavy frying pan, electric skillet or Chinese wok; heat to 370°. Fry burritos, three or four at a time, until puffy and golden on both sides, turning carefully, 2-1/2 to 3 minutes total. Remove with a slotted spoon and drain on paper towels. Serve hot, sifted with powdered sugar. Makes 12.

Flour tortillas: Mix 1-1/2 cups unsifted all-purpose flour and 3/4 teaspoon *each* salt and baking powder. Cut in 1 tablespoon lard until mixture is uniformly crumbly. Gradually mix in 1/3 to 1/2 cup cold water to make a soft dough. Divide dough into 12 equal portions; roll each into a small ball. Roll each out thinly on a well floured board or pastry cloth to a circle about 6 inches in diameter.

It's hard to resist some of the pastries and sweets offered by Mexican street vendors. These sweet tostadas are actually crisp caramel drizzled cookies, as made in Oaxaca.

Tortilla Press Cookies *(Tostadas Dulces de Oaxaca)*

2½ cups unsifted all-purpose flour
1 teaspoon baking powder
½ teaspoon *each* salt and cinnamon
⅔ cup sugar
⅓ cup *each* lard and firm butter
    or margarine
1 egg
1 teaspoon vanilla
1 tablespoon brandy, rum or
    orange juice
Caramelized sugar (directions
    follow)
Granulated sugar

In a large mixing bowl mix together flour, baking powder, salt, cinnamon and sugar. Cut in lard and butter until mixture forms coarse uniform crumbs. Beat together egg, vanilla and brandy. Add egg mixture, about 1 tablespoon at a time, mixing lightly with a fork after each addition, until dough clings together. Use your hands to press dough together. Pinch off pieces of dough and shape each into a ball about the size of a large walnut. Place pieces, one at a time, between sheets of waxed paper in a tortilla press, and press them flat (or, roll out, one at a time, with a rolling pin on a floured surface until they are about 1/8 inch thick). Remove top sheet of waxed paper. Place, cooky-side-down, on ungreased baking sheets and carefully peel off paper. Bake in a 375° oven for 7 to 10 minutes until golden brown. Arrange on cooling racks in a single layer. Working quickly, brush or drizzle cookies with hot caramelized sugar, then sprinkle lightly with granulated sugar. Makes about 20 large cookies (about 5 inches in diameter).

Caramelized sugar: Place 1/2 cup sugar in a small heavy frying pan over moderately high heat. Heat, tipping and tilting pan so sugar caramelizes evenly, until sugar is a deep amber color. If syrup cools and begins to harden, replace it over low heat until it is liquid again.

Pies as we know them north of the border certainly haven't been part of the Mexican menu for very long. But with such marvelous fresh fruits to put in them, the cross-cultural impulse must have been irresistible. One delightful result is this frozen fresh lime pie. The beaten egg white topping remains soft and easy to cut although the filling beneath it freezes firmly.

Frozen Lime Pie   *(Pastel de Limon)*

3   eggs, separated
1   can (14.oz.) sweetened condensed
      milk
1   teaspoon grated fresh lime peel
½   cup fresh lime juice
     Green food coloring (optional)
     Flaky Pastry (recipe follows)
⅛   teaspoon cream of tartar
¼   cup sugar

In a mixing bowl combine egg yolks, sweetened condensed milk, lime peel and lime juice. Beat with an electric mixer until smooth and thickened. Add a drop or two of green food coloring, if you wish. Spread in cooled pastry. Using a clean bowl and beaters, beat egg whites with cream of tartar until soft peaks form. Adding 1 tablespoon at a time, gradually beat in sugar, beating until whites are stiff and glossy. Spread over lime filling. Freeze until firm, 3 to 4 hours. Let stand at room temperature for 5 to 10 minutes before serving. Makes 6 to 8 servings.

Flaky Pastry: In a bowl mix 1 cup unsifted all-purpose flour and 1 tablespoon powdered sugar. Cut in 1/4 cup firm butter and 1 tablespoon lard until mixture forms coarse, uniform crumbs. Lightly mix in 1-1/2 to 2 tablespoons cold water, stirring until mixture clings together. Form dough into a ball. Roll out on a floured board or pastry cloth. Ease pastry into a 9-inch pie pan; trim and flute edge. With a fork, pierce pastry over bottom and sides. Bake in a 425° oven for 8 to 10 minutes, until lightly browned. Cool on a rack.

If you enjoy fresh pineapple, be sure to try one of these pies. The first has a meringue topping, and the other a golden top crust. The latter is delicious with vanilla ice cream.

Caribbean Fresh Pineapple Meringue Pie

1   medium-sized fresh pineapple
1¼ cups sugar
5   tablespoons cornstarch
1   tablespoon lime or lemon juice
3   egg yolks
2   tablespoons butter or margarine
1   cup boiling water
    Flaky Pastry (recipe follows)
    Meringue (recipe follows)

Peel pineapple and cut fruit into about 1/2-inch cubes; drain, reserving juices (you should have 3-1/2 to 4 cups fruit). In a 3-quart saucepan mix sugar and cornstarch. Blend in lime juice, pineapple juice and egg yolks until well combined. Add butter. Gradually add boiling water, stirring constantly. Bring to boiling, stirring constantly, over moderately high heat. Reduce heat as mixture begins to thicken; boil slowly for 1 minute. Fold in pineapple; stir over medium heat for 2 minutes. Spread filling in baked pastry shell. Let stand while preparing meringue. Place meringue atop warm filling in several mounds; using a narrow spatula, spread meringue gently to seal edges against crust, then in swirls toward center to cover pie evenly. Bake in a 350° oven for 10 to 12 minutes until meringue is golden brown. Cool on a wire rack. Makes 8 servings.

Flaky Pastry: Mix 1 cup unsifted all-purpose flour and 1 tablespoon powdered sugar. Cut in 1/4 cup firm butter and 1 tablespoon lard until mixture forms uniformly coarse crumbs. Lightly mix in 1-1/2 to 2 tablespoons cold water, stirring until mixture clings together. Form dough into a ball. Roll out on a floured board or pastry cloth. Ease pastry into a 9-inch pie pan; trim and flute edge. With a fork, pierce pastry over bottom and sides. Bake in a 425° oven for 8 to 10 minutes, until lightly browned. Cool on a rack.

Meringue: In a small bowl beat 3 egg whites with 1/8 teaspoon cream of tartar until soft peaks form. Adding 1 tablespoon at a time, gradually beat in 1/3 cup sugar, beating until whites are stiff and glossy.

Zihuatanejo Fresh Pineapple Pie   *(Pastel de Piña)*

2	eggs
1¼	cups sugar
2	tablespoons flour
	Juice of 1 small lime (about 1½ tablespoons)
4	cups fresh pineapple, cut in bite-sized pieces
	Flaky Pastry (recipe follows)
	Sugar

Beat eggs slightly; mix in sugar, flour and lime juice. Fold in pineapple and its juices. Roll out half of the pastry on a floured board or pastry cloth. Use it to line a 9-inch pie pan. Fill with pineapple mixture. Roll out remaining pastry. Place atop filling, trim and make a high fluted edge. Cut several decorative vents around center, or pierce with a fork in several places, to allow steam to escape. Sprinkle lightly with sugar. Bake in a 425° oven for 35 to 45 minutes, until top is browned and filling bubbles. Serve warm or at room temperature, with vanilla ice cream, if you wish. Makes 6 to 8 servings.

Flaky Pastry: Mix 2 cups unsifted all-purpose flour and 1/2 teaspoon salt. Cut in 1/3 cup firm butter and 1/4 cup lard until mixture forms coarse uniform crumbs. Using a fork, gradually add 2 to 3 tablespoons cold water, stirring lightly until mixture clings together. Divide in two equal portions, and shape each into a smooth ball.

Choosing a Fresh Pineapple

Perhaps you have heard that pulling on a pineapple leaf is a test of ripeness—the more readily the leaf can be removed, the riper the fruit.

A well known produce expert thinks the color of the skin is a better indication. If the outside color is yellow to golden orange, the fruit will be sweeter than that of a green pineapple. Once a pineapple is picked, sweetness will not increase as it does with other fruits, so it is best to find one that was picked fairly ripe.

Also try to avoid bruised or discolored pineapples or those with dry looking or brown leaves.

Finding, cracking and grating or shredding a fresh coconut is worth the trouble to make this devastatingly rich custard pie from Yucatán. A food processor or blender makes the grating easy.

Fresh Coconut Pie   *(Pastel de Coco)*

2 eggs
1 can (14 oz.) sweetened con-
       densed milk
1 teaspoon vanilla
2 cups grated fresh coconut (see
       note)
   Graham Cracker Crust (recipe
       follows)

Beat eggs until thick and pale; blend in condensed milk and vanilla. Mix in coconut. Pour into cooled, baked graham cracker crust. Bake in a 350° oven until filling is set and top is browned, 25 to 30 minutes. Serve warm or at room temperature. Makes 8 servings.

Graham Cracker Crust: Mix 1 cup fine graham cracker crumbs, 1/4 teaspoon cinnamon, 3 tablespoons sugar and 1/4 cup melted butter or margarine until well combined. Press graham cracker mixture evenly and firmly into a 9-inch pie pan. Bake in a 350° oven for 8 to 10 minutes, until firm and browned. Cool completely, for at least 1 hour.

Note: If fresh coconut is not available, you can substitute packaged, grated *unsweetened* coconut, which can be found in health food stores.

Cracking a Fresh Coconut

To open a fresh coconut, first puncture the eyes at the end of the coconut and drain off the liquid. Place coconut in a 350° oven for 30 minutes (outer shell will usually crack in several places). Open the hot coconut by placing it on a hard surface, such as a concrete floor or patio; hit it sharply with a hammer to split the shell. Pry out the coconut meat with a table knife. Remove the brown skin with a potato peeler. Rinse and dry coconut on paper towels, then grate or shred as you wish.

Finally, a two-layer cake with a fudge-like brown sugar and coffee frosting. With one layer vanilla and the other chocolate, it combines all the choicest Mexican dessert flavors.

Mexican Mocha Cake   *(Pastel de Moca)*

2   cups sifted all-purpose flour
1   tablespoon baking powder
1   teaspoon salt
½   cup (¼ lb.) soft butter or
      margarine
1   cup sugar
1   teaspoon vanilla
2   eggs
¾   cup milk
1   tablespoon unsweetened cocoa
      Mocha Caramel Frosting (recipe
      follows)

Grease two 8-inch round baking pans; line with waxed paper (grease paper also) and lightly flour, tapping to remove excess. Sift together flour, baking powder and salt; set aside. In a large bowl, cream butter and sugar until light and fluffy; blend in vanilla. Beat in eggs, one at a time. Add flour mixture to creamed mixture alternately with milk, beginning and ending with flour. Beat well after each addition. Spread half of the batter in one of the prepared pans. Beat cocoa into remaining batter until well combined; spread that batter in second pan. Bake in a 350° oven for 30 to 35 minutes, until cake pulls away from sides of pan and springs back when touched lightly. Cool in pans on wire racks for 10 minutes, then turn out onto racks to complete cooling. Fill and spread sides and top with Mocha Caramel Frosting. Makes 1 cake.

Mocha Caramel Frosting: Melt 1/2 cup (1/4 lb.) butter or margarine in a 2-quart saucepan; stir in 1 cup firmly packed light brown sugar, 2 teaspoons instant coffee powder or crystals and 1 teaspoon unsweetened cocoa. Bring to boiling and boil vigorously, stirring constantly, for 2 minutes. Remove from heat and add 1/4 cup milk, stirring vigorously. Replace over heat and again bring to a full boil. Remove from heat and let cool until lukewarm, about 20 minutes. Stir in 1/2 teaspoon vanilla and 2 cups sifted powdered sugar, beating until smooth, thick and cool enough to spread.

METRIC CONVERSION TABLE

U.S. Measure	Metric Measure ***
Liquid Measure:	
1/4 teaspoon	1.25 milliliters (ml.)
1/2 teaspoon	2.5 milliliters
3/4 teaspoon	3.75 milliliters
1 teaspoon	5 milliliters
1 tablespoon	15 milliliters
1 fluid ounce	30 milliliters
1 fluid ounce	.03 liter (l.)
1/4 cup	.06 liter
1/2 cup	.12 liter
3/4 cup	.18 liter
1 cup	.236 liter
1 pint	.473 liter
1 quart	.946 liter
1 gallon	3.785 liters

Temperatures:

200° Fahrenheit	93° Celsius
225°	107°
250°	121°
275°	135°
300°	149°
325°	163°
350°	177°
375°	191°
400°	205°
425°	218°
450°	232°
475°	246°
500°	260°

Dry Bulk — Weight

Metric equivalents to U.S. dry bulk measures are not listed here as dry materials (such as flour and sugar) are measured in weight, not bulk, under the metric system. For example: 1 cup all-purpose flour equals 115 grams; 1 cup granulated white sugar weighs 200 grams.

1 ounce	28.5 grams (g.)
1 pound	2.2046 kilograms (kg.)

***Amounts given are approximate